FROM MILLENNIALS WITH LOVE

Young professional's stories on their experience of work

Collective work coordinated by

Ann-Victoire Pincé

FastPrint Publishing

http://www.fast-print.net/bookshop

FROM MILLENNIALS WITH LOVE

YOUNG PROFESSIONALS' STORIES ON THEIR EXPERIENCE OF WORK

A catalogue record for this book is available from the British Library

ISBN 978-178456-247-2

First published 2015 by
FASTPRINT PUBLISHING
Peterborough, England.

To

Antoine & Saúl

Acknowledgements

This book has benefited from the help and support of many which I would like to thank today. In particular, I would like to thank Teju Jhaveri for her creativity and responsiveness in graphic design, and Greg Kuzdenyi for his guidance and coaching in building our website. Many thanks to Toru Jhaveri for running several interviews, and being a great partner in bouncing back ideas. A big thank you to Eidi Cruz and Matthew Smith in the final review of the manuscript. 'Merci' to François Meillant for his encouragements and continuous support during this journey.

Contents

FROM MILLENNIALS WITH LOVE

Preface: A few words of introduction

'Man(kind) is the only true source of wealth'
Jean Bodin (1577)[1]

Nineteen-eighty-nine was a busy year for my mother. Joining a company she had to quickly get up to speed on a topic that she did not master at the time. For a few weeks, she brought work at home and spent her evenings teaching herself the basics of the industry she had just entered: information technologies. In particular, she had to better understand the language engineers used for coding, which required using her personal computer. What that meant was that when my mother had to bring work home, she literally brought 'work' home and that was hard work in itself. Remember those ancient times when personal computers were impossible to carry around, at the risk of breaking your back, and if you wanted to take on that risk, they could hardly fit into your car.

I am currently working on a computer that is just over 1 kilogram and I find it heavy already, but back in the eighties, computers were substantially different in terms of size and weight. They were

---

[1] Bodin, J. (1577) Les six livres de la République, Paris.

just not as mobile. The entire family needed to be involved in helping the transition from work to home: one to carry the 12" screen – which of course had a frame just as large around it; another one taking care of the tower, a third one for the keyboard, mouse and other accessories and cables. If your arms were long enough to carry your computer screen alone – mine never were – you would size this massive screen, due to the weight and lack of visibility, were forced into making very small steps, jumping left then right, and basically looked like an old grumpy bear. No wonder why at the time, people avoided bringing work at home too frequently.

When I think back about what I have observed and stories I have heard of my parents' working lives, I realise the amplitude of the revolution we have undergone, or I should say, are undergoing. And this is what lies at the heart of the stories we would like to share in this book.

This book is a collection of personal stories about how young professionals see and experience work, reflecting the realities in which we evolve today. Those stories touch on topics such as the challenges and opportunities of starting to work at the beginning of one of the most important economic crises of the last hundred years; what do we want, as young professionals, from our work, our manager, our CEO and organisation; how do we think about what it means to work; or how do we envisage the world of work evolving tomorrow.

We do not pretend to give any general truths, but rather personal perspectives. Our only interest here is to share our stories, hoping to open up a conversation. Although some of the contributors of this book are academics, the narratives you will find are little grounded in research. Rather, they are grounded in experience.

The book has developed as a conversation itself, which is reflected in its structure. It is organised around five narratives, each focusing on different aspects of the contributors' working experiences. After completion, each narrative was shared with another person involved in this initiative, and discussed during a one on one interview. Narratives and interviewees were matched based on their interests, experiences and backgrounds. Those interviews sometimes went a little off topic and became a platform to discuss work experiences at large, yet we have decided to keep them verbatim and to amend them as little as possible.

We then have in total ten individuals who contributed to this journey, constituting a fairly diverse group. Contributors are either living or coming from the following countries: Chile, China, France, Germany, Hungary, Iceland, India, Israel, Mexico, the Netherlands, Switzerland, the UK. However, we have more in common than what this cultural diversity seems to suggest. We are all organisational psychologists who studied at the same school, enrolled in the same program. We went to the London School of Economics, following the MSc of Organisational and Social Psychology, and graduated between 2007 and 2008. More importantly, we share a passion for organisational life and a perspective on how to look at it.

We have another point in common that is important to note: we are very lucky people. How to describe the opportunity of education differently? And this is probably where our personal accounts of organisational life are biased and raise primarily the questions of the 'lucky' ones, or in other words, those who have a choice. This brings some partiality in our stories and it seems imperative to me to stress that what we discuss here might not reflect the reality of the majority.

Now, how has this idea come about? Well, the idea of this book finds its origins in my own experience of acculturation. Despite the fact that I was born and raised in France, from the age of four until I reached eighteen, I went to a German school and left the country to finish my studies abroad in an Anglo-Saxon environment where I ended up staying for six full years. Over the years, being exposed to different cultures, ways of being, thinking and relating to one another, I have felt less and less French, and increasingly a citizen of the world. I experienced and integrated Anglo-Saxon ways of working, management style and working life patterns. When moving back to France a couple of years ago, I started reading about French organisations and the local business culture. One of the books I read at the time 'shocked' me culturally speaking. Reading through this book hurt my ideals, my vision of the world and my hopes for organisational life. This book was negative, portrayed organisations as fully dysfunctional and allowed for no improvement perspectives. What was so surprising to me was not so much the message – the author, of course, had full rights to express his views of organisations – but the impact of this message. The book was granted awards, rated highly by the press as well as by readers. The pathos of the depressed organisation seemed to resonate with readers. It did not with me. Frustration levels rising with every line read, I started discussing the matter with a few people around me. It emerged from those initial exchanges that what was described in that book may have been particularly anchored in the realities of the French context, and that a more international account would bring a different light. It also appeared that my perspective may have been biased by the specificities of the generation I belong to, the so-called Generation Y, bringing a more optimistic view to organisations.

This initiative then started in reaction to that book, with the desire of giving a positive account of organisational life. Reality is of course more complicated, and we ended up with stories about our experiences of work, both positive and negative.

I am now going to briefly describe how the book is structured, and in order to better understand the cultural diversity of the accounts provided in this document, I will highlight where our contributors come from.

In the first part, Patrizia Hoyer shares her journey in finding her balance between money, magic and meaning at work, first as a management consultant, and then as a doctorate student. Patrizia lives in Switzerland but is actually German and has Bangladeshi origins. Her narrative was then discussed with Johannes Froehlich, another German citizen, who has been living in the UK for over ten years.

Our second part takes us to Latin America. Eidi Cruz, who is from Mexico and lives in between Mexico City and London, explores the essence and definition of how work may be understood, and anchors her narrative in her geographical and historical contexts. The interview to discuss this narrative was conducted with Manuel Riveros, who is Chilean and has been living in Europe for numerous years.

The third part of our journey continues to India. In her narrative, Toru Jhaveri discusses her search for appropriate levels of passion at work and the importance to put work into perspective, understanding work as just one part of life. She then discussed her narrative with Daphna Salomon, who is Israeli and living in London.

In a four part, Jen Lu details her experience of working in academia, bringing particular light on the difficulties she faced starting to work at the beginning of a major economic crisis. Although living in London for a few years now, Jen is Dutch and has Chinese roots. Ása, who lives in Iceland, was then interviewed to further discuss her narrative.

In a final part, I share my experience of finding the right professional fit, enabling me to fully engage in my work. As described above, I am now back in France, my home country, after having spent a few years abroad. I then discussed my account with Greg Kuzdenyi who lives in London and has Hungarian origins.

In the Postface, we conclude with a few words to recap on what appears to come through the different narratives and interviews, and hope to open up a conversation with other young professionals, HR practitioners, business leaders and those generally interested in the topic. One of our main focuses in this initiative is to provide a starting point to exchange on what the world of work feels like today, and we would very much welcome your perspective on the matter. If you wanted to join the conversation, don't hesitate to visit our website: www.frommillennialswithlove.com

Ann-Victoire Pincé

PART1:

Money, Magic & Meaning

In Search of Money, Magic and Meaning

Patrizia Hoyer

When I was just a little girl, I asked my mother:
"What will I be? Will I be pretty? Will I be rich?"
Here's what she said to me:
"Que sera, sera, whatever will be, will be.
The future's not ours to see, que sera sera,
what will be, will be."
Ray Evans & Jay Livingston (1956)[2]

A few words on Patrizia

Patrizia is currently a post-doctoral scholar at the Research Institute of Organisational Psychology at the University Of Saint Gallen, Switzerland. Her research interests include discursive and narrative approaches to identity, elite working contexts, power and resistance, local affiliations along global career paths, cosmopolitan theory, creativity and social/organisational change. Patrizia holds a PhD in Organisational Studies and Cultural Theory from the University of Saint Gallen. Prior to her doctoral work, she worked as a strategy consultant for a global management consultancy in Zurich.

---

[2] Evans, R. & Livingston, J. (1956). Que sera sera.

Patrizia bring along a diversity of cross-cultural experiences. This includes her Bangladeshi family background, her upbringing and school education in Germany, her university studies in London, as well as her work and academic experience in Switzerland. This wealth of diverse experiences has increased her appreciation of difference and keeps her hungry for new explorations.

Some years ago I received two gifts from a fellow student of mine at the LSE, a lady in her late forties (even though you would never have guessed), who has had 25 years of work experience as an independent organisational change consultant. The first gift I received from her is one beyond price and measure, namely the gift of friendship. The second one appears to be just as long-lasting as the first, a piece of wisdom on professional life that I have ironically decided to prove wrong. By sharing with you this piece of wisdom I hope to better explain what I personally look for, both in my aspired academic career as well as in my research as organisational psychologist.

'When looking for a job', my friend explained, 'it is close to impossible to find something which combines those three components that matter most: Money, magic and meaning. If you are lucky', she asserted, 'you will find a job that gives you two. A lot of people survive on even just one.' If you do the little math, you will find this to be a simple truth. Even though I don't want to make too simplistic a categorization of jobs, I do feel that giving examples brings life to the discussion.

Let's start with the notion of meaning. To my understanding a job that is (above all) meaningful is one that allows you to be of help to others, to make a change, to have an impact. Examples of these kinds of professions would be nurses, firemen or people working for NGOs. The notion of magic in professional life is probably more difficult to be put in words. Magic to me means waking up in the morning – happily – and just knowing, whilst leaving the house to go to work, that you are 'on the right way'. When you have found magic in your work – and if you have please count yourself lucky – you do not consider it a service that you render to an employer, but rather your satisfaction comes from the work or its outcome itself. Working with children can for example be magical, as children, without even knowing, give so much back to the person who takes loving care. Or artists - isn't their work all about magic? Don't they get mystified, absorbed, completely carried away in their assignments?

This sounds so ideal, I would argue, that in line with some managerial literature on job motivation one could not care less about money. And indeed, most of this research on motivation focuses on the aspects of good leadership and intrinsic rewards in the realm of magic and meaning, downplaying the role of money altogether. As a proponent of extrinsic rewards, however, I would argue that this 'money, no thanks!-attitude' is rather outdated. More than ever, university graduates compare remuneration packages and flock to those jobs that pay best, happily agreeing to 'sell their souls'. And despite greatest moral accusations and finger pointing, managers insist on large bonuses; a behaviour that has not changed significantly even in times of financial crises.

Given the unprecedented financial crisis that we have just experienced, however, I have to admit that this entire debate around job characteristics almost feels misplaced, signifying a 'luxury problem' in times of large scale downsizing, companies filing for bankruptcy and emerging waves of suicide. And without wanting to disrespect these developments that I have been following with great concern, I would still like to hold on to my seemingly unshakable optimism with regards to the next 35 years of my prospective working life.

In my optimistic vision I will eventually end my career with a strike of perfect balance between the three ingredients for a happy life. And as I keep this grand final in mind, on my current journey I am already in negotiation with myself and my work environment to constantly search for, play around with and where possible engage in some optimizing activity regarding this money, magic and meaning triad.

To give you a very short version of the status quo: Yes, I have found magic in the work that I do. It even feels so magical sometimes that I can hardly view it as 'real work' so that money (which of course I need!) simply becomes a nice add-on. I have thought for long, very naively to be fair, that money is not an issue in academia, that it is just a matter of 'not too good' and 'not too bad', just fine to make a happy living. Now I have learned that at universities, just like in other organisations, resources in forms of university budgets and external project-funding are limited and have to be heavily fought for. While this is not yet an issue for me personally, it is one that I am also observing with unease and alarm.

So when looking at my 'money, magic, meaning' balance I would say that money is just fine (particularly since time for writing is so scarce in academia that it is 'worth more' than the extra money I could get for additional teaching), magic has exceeded all my expectations while meaning-making will continue to be an on-going endeavour.

A former 'money, magic meaning' balance that I have encountered in my previous job marks the diametrical opposite to what I am experiencing now: In management consulting there is plenty of money, no magic in the work itself (as it is mainly number crunching, especially at the bottom of the pyramid), and the issue of meaning remains controversial, even though according to Furusten (2009)[3] 'management consulting is of more use for organisations at least than management science is' (p. 265). I will not follow up on this claim by Furusten, but instead I will give my own personal account of how I experienced these working contexts of management consulting and academia and let you decide for yourself on their potential for providing money, magic and meaning.

My experience as management consultant

"The highest reward for a man's toil is not what he gets for it, but what he becomes by it." (John Ruskin, 1819-1900)

My first job right after graduation was a position as strategy consultant in a renowned global management consultancy. I probably joined the consulting industry for the same reasons that many graduates do: to become part of this supposedly 'hard

[3] Furusten, S. (2009). Management consultants as improvising agents of stability. Scandinavian Journal of Management, 25(3), 264–274.

working and clever elite', while at the same time trying to stay immune to the so-called 'brainwashing techniques' applied in management consultancies. When considering two particular mechanisms used in management consultancies for controlling the behaviour of their employees – constructing a self-pleasing image of elite and maintaining certain levels of insecurity – I have to admit that these instruments of domination worked perfectly well for me. When trying to make retrospective sense of my consulting experience, it would be very tempting of course to portray myself as a heroic survivor who has elegantly defied all forces of organisational domination. This, however, would be nothing but a distorted narrative, rooted in what Lacan has labelled mere 'fantasy' (Driver, 2009)[4].

Instead, when reconstructing my personal experience as management consultant, I will try not to embellish things too much. At the same time I would ask the reader to kindly grant me some space for 'face-saving activities' in my account, just so that I may be at peace with myself. For most of the time in my 18 months as management consultant (which in hindsight feel more like several years), I was never really at ease in my position. While I had hoped that I could bring in my knowledge as a graduate in Organisational Psychology, I soon found out that I was mainly hired for analysing financial reports, for number crunching, and for producing fancy, yet standardized PowerPoint decks. This was not what I had anticipated or desired from my first job. The compensation was ridiculously good though. Before I had even started on the job, the company had paid my moving expenses

---

[4] Driver, M. (2009). From Loss to Lack: Stories of Organisational Change as Encounters with Failed Fantasies of Self, Work and Organisation. Organisation, 16(3), 353-369.

from Germany to Switzerland, had asked me to pick up my brand new car, my laptop, my mobile phone. This was all before I had worked even for a single day. And also my monthly salary was much higher than what I could have easily spent in a month.

All this appeared overly generous. But on my third day on the job I was staffed on a project and for the next nine months I never got to leave the office before midnight, at least not from Monday to Thursday. And on weekends, junior consultants had to do a financial news screening for the partners of the firm, so that they could identify potential for new business. Interestingly, the long working hours were not even my problem, but I did feel a strong pressure to perform and I felt I was being constantly monitored. Another big issue was that I was not really happy or fulfilled in doing the tasks I was given, and so I soon shifted focus and did more of that, what an organisational psychologist would do more naturally. I started to observe people.

I was pretty amazed with and soon became preoccupied with the question of how people 'function' in management consultancies. I observed that most consultants functioned exceptionally well in fact, some of them (even though not the majority) staying 5, 10 or even more than 15 years in the consultancy. I found that each consultant had developed a strategy for survival and I would roughly divide survival strategies into two different camps. One way of surviving would be to fully buy into the promoted corporate culture, take up the company's 'DNA' (the metaphor my previous employer used for promoting a shared organisational identity) and to become, in a more cynical reading, a complete corporate clone.

Even though one would find consultants of that mind-set to complain every now and then about the extremes of their work assignments, that is, long working hours, meticulous performance monitoring, deadline pressures and no sleep, these 'war-stories' would often still fall into a self-image-boosting-strategy for letting the others know about their own toughness. The other camp of survivors was made up of people who would partially buy into the organisationally defined identity, but at times (some more frequently than others) would escape the normalizing gaze and develop strategies of subtle resistance. Due to limited space I will only focus on one of these strategies here which I found particularly intriguing for resisting some of the imperatives for organisational identification: the refuge to 'protective friendships'.

It was due to these protective friendships, I would claim, that I stayed in the consulting industry for 18 months instead of just one (especially since I had my first conversation with HR about quitting after just five weeks into the job). I acknowledge that the mention of friendship in a professional context is rather uncommon, as this is regarded a private matter that does not belong into the sphere of the public. Friendship, in fact, is by definition set apart in the literature from relationships among family members, sexual partners or 'just work colleagues' (Grey & Sturdy, 2007)[5]. While there might be some tolerance for friendship among colleagues of the same hierarchical level, close friendship among superiors and subordinates becomes unthinkable however, as this may threaten or compromise organisational roles. Such constellations are only justified when friendship, in line with a humanistic style of management, becomes instrumentalized as a form of relationship

---

[5] Grey, C., & Sturdy, A. (2007). Friendship and Organisational Analysis: Toward a Research Agenda. Journal of Management Inquiry, 16(2), 157-172.

building which then again marks another tactic for exercising control (Kärreman & Alvesson, 2009)[6].

So much being said, particularly on the notion of separating friendship from the work context, I would argue that in my time working as a consultant, I learned more about the gift of friendship than I did about discounted cash flows, excel shortcuts, inventory optimization or 'winning in an economic downturn' strategies. Without obvious reasons or promises of personal gain, there were suddenly people in an overly hostile environment who offered unrequested and yet much appreciated support across different life and job challenges. While I could interpret this to be in line with the corporate culture's claim that 'a consultant never lets another consultant fail', there were clear indications that friendship became actually a way of protecting colleagues from the company's outrages demands on them, thus marking the emancipation from corporate culture rather than adherence to it.

Particularly in an up-or-out culture, where principles of 'natural selection' and 'survival of the fittest' dominate, traces of altruism can be expected to be absent. And yet, in several instances I have observed how individuals from same but also from different hierarchical levels have gone out of their way to help others with difficult tasks, to take positive influence on performance reviews or to actively protect particularly the 'young' consultants, who are most vulnerable to the up-or-out principle, from potential top-down abusiveness.

---

[6] Kärreman, D., & Alvesson, M. (2009). Resisting resistance: Counter-resistance, consent and compliance in a consultancy firm. Human Relations, 62(8), 1115-1144.

I would argue that protective friendship provided a source for dis- or counter-identification among those who offered and received help. Through bonds of friendship, people found a trusted group of colleagues with whom they could create, share and exchange narratives that were different and sometimes in opposition to the dominant discourses circulated in the consultancy. While the primary organisational discourses revolve around themes of competence development and careerism (Kärreman & Alvesson, 2009)[7], protective friendships could help people to set limits to mere performance thinking and to regain some control over their own life and future again.

Interestingly I observed that these bonds of friendship were stronger and more enduring than the imperatives for organisational identification. Especially when consultants left the company and looked back nostalgically to the past (Sturdy & Wright, 2008)[8], they did little to stay in touch with the company itself, for example through official alumni events. At the same time, ex-consultants strongly maintained and fostered the friendships that have sheltered and protected them from agonizing techniques of control. So even today, to be a living example, I consider some of my past consulting colleagues to be my closest friends – still now, four and a half years after leaving the consultancy.

To round-up my experience as management consultant, it should not come as a surprise that after 18 months of number crunching and the generation of PowerPoint decks I left the consultancy to do

---

[7] Kärreman, D., & Alvesson, M. (2009). Resisting resistance: Counter-resistance, consent and compliance in a consultancy firm. Human Relations, 62(8), 1115-1144.

[8] Sturdy, A., & Wright, C. (2008). A Consulting Diaspora? Enterprising Selves as Agents of Enterprise. Organisation, 15(3), 427-444.

more of that work again, which I really love: Being an organisational psychologist, being a researcher, and dedicating my research to a subject that I really find puzzling even today: 'The ambiguous identity constructions of (former) management consultants'.

My experience as doctoral student, researcher, and teaching assistant

I ask the forgiveness of all students who may read this chapter for dedicating it to a professor. I have a serious reason: I consider this professor to have a student's heart. I have another reason: this professor understands everything, even the concerns of students. I have a third reason: He is the most modest professor I have ever met. If all these reasons are not enough, I will dedicate this paper to the student that he once was. All professors were once students (although few of them remember it). And so I correct my dedication:

TO MY PROFESSOR WHEN HE WAS A STUDENT

Chris Steyaert. An unusual name. Creativity, Gender and Reflexivity. Not the topics I would expect nor be particularly interested in to investigate. And yet an organisational psychologist. After all that's what I want to be. Why not give it (him) a try? Our first meeting, which is also my job interview, is rather 'special'. My counterpart seems rather shy, which I didn't expect of a professor.

I try some small talk but he remains rather reactive if not to say passive. Overall a strange and slightly alienating set-up. The questions he asks, however, are sharp and to the point. He wants me to reflect about things right there and then. 'Does change always require some degree of reflexivity?' 'What are the shortcomings of Moscovici's theory on social representations?' He really pushes for an answer. He himself says very little and the way he speaks is quiet, not really firm. But what he says leaves an impression. Quite an impression.

Three weeks into the job I am asked to assist in the teaching of an MBA course on Creativity in Organisations. Two days before the start of the course the professor admits to me that he is a bit 'scared'. I find this very confusing. Why would a professor be scared? Should I be scared too? Then on the first day of the course I arrive early. He is already in the classroom. Very quiet. Very concentrated. Creating an aura of 'don't talk to me'. I don't. I sit and wait and watch. The lesson starts. My lesson starts. The moment that the class is opened I have the feeling that I have never been in a classroom before. That never before I had an idea of what a lecture could be. Of what a professor could be. Never before had I met Chris Steyaert.

The reason why I refer to these early encounters with my 'Doktorvater' is to draw attention to the creative inspirations which these experiences provided me with. When Twyla Tharp (2008)[9], a famous dance choreographer speaks of learning from others, she gives the example of Brahms, who until his mid-forties could not get out his first symphony as he was so respectful of, in a way humbled or even intimidated by the greatness of other composers

---

[9] Tharp, T. (2008) Creativity step by step. Harvard Business Review, 86(4), 47-51.

such as Beethoven. I can relate to that example very well. When I first experienced this person in action, I was truly enchanted by his way of teaching. But it did not take long until I felt a heavy burden in acknowledging that there are years of experience between me and such a well-staged performance, and more shockingly, that it might not only be years that separate me from achieving such eloquence. However, what Tharp argues is that not trying to bring out one's own 'composition' (such as in the case of Brahms), just because others will always be better, bears a certain arrogance in itself. The learning I took from that is not to worry too much about measuring up to the giants, but to take one step at a time, be inspired by the teachings and writings of others and to learn through failure.

And yet, coming back to the earlier notion of magic, I do want to share some of the 'magic tricks' that I have learned from my professor over the past few years. Business schools, perhaps even more than other educational institutions, are often driven by a certain sense of 'functionality', where knowledge creation is regarded a rationalistic act that is disembodied and free of passion. Students no longer attend classes for the sake of learning something, but instead, they are most focused on getting the best 'return' on their education, that is, a highly paid job.

To counter a bit this development, I have learned from my professor what it means to introduce an 'anti-pedagogy' (Dey & Steyaert, 2007)[10], that is an 'atmosphere of excitement' (Whitehead, 1932)[11] into the classroom where strong views are

---

[10] Dey, P. & Steyaert, C. (2007) The troubadours of knowledge: passion and invention in management education. Organisation, 14(3), 437-461.

[11] Whitehead, A. N. (1932) The Aims of Education and other Essays. NY: The Free Press

expressed in a genuine love for wisdom, imagination as well as risk-taking. By (re-)introducing such passion into the classroom it will hopefully be possible to break some of the existing limits in teaching curricula and to cultivate a more holistic understanding of 'knowing through all senses' instead (Dey & Steyaert, 2007)[12].

So the first and most basic step I have learned in my role as teaching assistant is to transform a class room, or more importantly, the students who usually inhabit it. I learned for example how to make students – including Bachelor, Master and MBA students – dance, sing and act in the classroom. After students recover from the first shock of not being allowed to use PowerPoint in their presentations, they soon get intrigued about learning other ways of expressing themselves, while a highlight of the course remains a three-hour improvisation training with a professional dance choreographer.

And to not only 'preach' but also experiment myself with some of these alternative forms of expressing myself, I have dared to try out different things when presenting part of my research. I recount that once, in a doctoral course at the University of St. Gallen for instance I gave a performance on my PhD project which was as bizarre as the location of its presentation. The performance itself consisted of a bricolage of 19th century love poetry, recruitment talk, provocative images of suffering and abuse and a 15 minutes video of a person vomiting. The carefully chosen location: a public ladies' toilet at the university, which for the time of the presentation – and probably for the better – was in fact closed to the public. In sheer contrast to that I remember my attempt to

[12] Dey, P. & Steyaert, C. (2007) The troubadours of knowledge: passion and invention in management education. Organisation, 14(3), 437-461.

appear nothing but professional when presenting part of my PhD at the 73rd Annual Meeting of the Academy of Management in Orlando, Florida, where the only dubiousness of my presentation could possibly have come from the conference venue at the heart of Disney World. I found it important to not only learn one form of presenting, but to have a broad repertoire that can be activated across different locations and situations.

Also in the written versions of my PhD work I have experimented with different genres and writing styles. This ranged from what has been referred to as 'playful fairy-tale writing' to the aspiration of producing publishable work for highly ranked and peer reviewed journals. In my fairy-tale writing I attempted, among other things, to describe my own PhD journey along metaphors of arranged marriage, love affairs, promiscuity and long-lasting romance; a narrative which did not spare its readers from the kinky details of my PhD fantasies. Quite differently, when writing for journals, I tried to be rather dry and detached in my narrative to better match the overall tone of these outlets.

To share some of my broader research philosophy as well, I do not assume that research ever comes out in a fully formed way. Instead I would consider it a piece of art that requires various acts of engagement such as reading, observing, stepping back and reflecting. Simultaneously, making sense of experience occurs through activities of writing, dismissing and rewriting. It is a process of working and reworking (Gartner, 2011)[13] until some level of satisfaction sets in. And yet, just like in the arts, it would be misleading to ever think of a piece of academic writing as being

---

[13] Gartner, W. (2011) When words fail: An entrepreneurship glossolalia. Entrepreneurship & Regional Development: An International Journal, 23(1-2), 9-21.

'finished'. More accurately, it is always in the making. Likewise, the role of researcher is also in a steady process of becoming. Assuming that there cannot be scholarship without a scholar, Hancock and Tyler (2008)[14] state that identity-making itself, rather than being a matter of authenticity or inauthenticity, can also be considered a creative activity of producing oneself as a work of art that must meet certain 'aesthetic values' and 'stylistic criteria'. That means that not only academic writing or output is reframed as art, but the researcher herself, in the artistic process of creation, invents a new image of 'self'.

In all this I learned that if there is one thing, which can bring true satisfaction and happiness into my personal workplace, it is the permission to be creative and to engage in what Statler et al. (2011)[15] refer to as 'serious play'. According to Winnicott (1974)[16], play is something we particularly find in the early years of life when creating our own secret spaces that are both real and unreal, some places under the trees endowed with imagination. As we grow older, however, and as we enter formal education to tailor our lives towards a profession, we deprive ourselves gradually from the ability to play and thus the ability to develop creative spaces. And yet, such creative spaces, I would argue, are particularly important – even in the workplace. Especially after the economic crisis has depicted a breakdown of standard management tools, managers are systematically seeking for alternative logics and new ways of

---

14 Hancock, P. & Tyler, M. (2008) It's all too beautiful: Emotion and organisation in the aesthetic economy. In Fineman, S. (Ed.) The emotional organisation. Blackwell Publishing: Malden, MA.

15 Statler, M., Heracleuous, L. and Jacobs, C.D. (2011). Serious play as a practice of paradox. Journal of Applied Behavioral Science, 47(2), 236-256.

16 Winnicott, D. W. (1974). Playing and reality. Harmondsworth, UK: Penguin.

organizing, among other things strongly incorporating creativity. For me, creative freedom has become the answer to be happy in my working life. It provides both magic and meaning, and just enough money to take care of all other matters.

Discussing the narrative with Johannes Froehlich

"If I could work three days as a consultant, one day doing something charitable, and one day doing something more artistic, that would be ideal"

A few words on Johannes

Johannes is Head of Integration & Advice at Business in the Community (BITC). BITC is the UK Prince's Responsible Business Network and stands for responsible business. The Integration and Advice team comprises three areas covering bespoke advisory services, benchmarking and training. Advisory Services delivers projects and advice to companies ranging from entirely bespoke advisory work to repeating products such as CR Index-based private benchmarks. The CR Index is a robust benchmarking tool developed in consultation with business leaders, to help companies systematically measure, manage and integrate responsible business practice. BITC's training services have been developed for practitioners who are looking to deepen their knowledge of Corporate Responsibility and develop essential competencies. In this leadership role Johannes is responsible for the successful implementation of the Integration and Advice team strategy in order to deliver a balanced budget and increase the impact of services to companies.

In his previous role as a senior consultant at IBM's Smarter Workforce division, Johannes worked on a variety of large scale and highly complex global leadership and engagement programmes to the highest of standards analysing business needs and providing solutions based on analytics and insights.

Interview transcripts

Interviewer: To start with, could you please tell us what you did when you left the London School of Economics?

Johannes Froehlich (JF): When I left the LSE, I started working on planning and organising the second Annual Global Management Summit of the Indian Institute of Management Alumni Association Europe in London. It was a conference on the topic of 'business changes in the light of globalisation'. This lasted only a few months before I found my current job but I enjoyed project managing and securing high profile speakers from both the business and academic worlds. Today, I work for a management consultancy where I lead and consult on a variety of large scale and highly complex global leadership and engagement programmes[17]. I plan project milestones and resources, analysing business needs, reviewing current programmes and initiatives and providing solutions based on a range of methodologies and tools. I lead the

---

[17] Since the interview, Johannes' has moved on to a different organisation.

strategic planning which involves designing and tailoring the adequate programme approach and related communication strategy to ensure consistent messaging, engaging and managing stakeholder relationships, and implementing governance structures to ensure sustainability. I wanted to work for a people and change company, not too big, and find a place where I felt I could apply what I had studied at the LSE. I wanted to find a place aligned with my thinking. What we focused on at the LSE was to avoid looking at organisations as static entities, but rather, to identify processes that are shaping those organisations. We were not interested in tangible things as such, but in what is happening, taking place, in the 'spaces in between'. What was important to me as well, was to work for a company where I feel that I can make a difference. We are working with such a large number of organisations, we have a real potential to impact the way those organisations actually function and to challenge them on the impact they have on their environment, on the communities in which they operate. I believe it is my role, as a consultant to work with them and advise them on how to position themselves, how to act responsibly. This is actually something I learnt going to a conference. There was one session on organisational psychology related to the environment where they clearly stated it was our responsibility to look at the wider context. We need to broaden our thinking. It is not just about organisations cut off from the environment, being inward focused, just looking at their employees, but it is also looking outwards, looking at the market, consumers, the macrocosm, how they are connected to it. It is all in relation to something. The world is increasingly more globalised, we cannot look at thing as disconnected any longer, but need to look at interconnectivities between organisations and their wider environment. They are part of that and cannot be exempt from all our global challenges, especially since organisations are, partly, a cause of those issues. But they can also be the solution to some of those challenges. So that is why I think we have a broader responsibility and role to play. When I say we, I am primarily talking about people working in our type of consultancies since it is about workforce, workforce science, organisations and people in organisations. But also, it is employees. As employees, we have a responsibility to demand more from our employers to be more responsible. And that is true for every employee of course. There are many discourses, and for the last few years, some are saying that the new generation is willing to work for organisations that are more responsible, but how much does that really translate into practice? There is a lot of talk but it does not really seem to be put into practice. We have been talking about CSR for years now and it is still not very tangible. There are projects here and there but we find a lot of 'green washing', but it is not much talked about in the board room, it is not part of the strategy so much, but it could be. This is part of our responsibility, as a consultancy, to talk and address these; designing the employer brand and attract customers and employees. Our responsibility is also to understand how this is really impacting talent retention, how important it is to employees. If it is important for talent, then how does that translate into hard figures? What needs to be done and really be applied in practice?

Interviewer: You are talking about to which extent CSR is impacting how employees may select an employer. Beyond what data could tell us, what have you experienced personally? Is that important to you? Did it play a role in selecting your organisation or in retaining you?

JF: For me personally, yes, it is important. If it is for others, I don't know. It did not impact my decision so much when I started working in this company but certainly going forward it will, and also in the recent past, it was important to me. When I had an offer to work for a tobacco company, I said no. This is not something I would be proud to do. Is that slightly hypocritical? Yeah, maybe, if I google most of the companies I am working with, I can always find something that is unethical. I can make a case, saying that at least it is a good place to start a dialogue with those organisations. But clearly a tobacco company is a totally different game, because their product is not something that I can stand behind.

Interviewer: In terms of the behaviours you have seen in your organisation, is there anything that showed you that your company was or not socially responsible?

JF: I don't really see any evidence of either. I don't see them as particularly ethical or unethical. I don't see them doing anything wrong but I don't think they are doing anything particularly proactive in having programs that would be part of the culture, our DNA, the way we do things and what we stand for. I don't see that either. Would I like to see more of that? Yes, absolutely. For me, personally, it would be a driver in making a decision to work for an organisation that is responsible. I want to make a distinction between being ethical and the work that we do. If the work that we do has an impact in that direction, that is a motivation for me to leave or join an organisation. If an organisation is directly touching those points, that would be very attractive to me.

Interviewer: That nicely leads to the narrative that Patrizia has written and the triangle around meaning, magic and money, and particularly on the notion of meaning. I would like to ask you, how would you define this notion of meaning?

JF: I think there are several aspects to it. Meaning to me is really related to the content of the work we do. Personally, work is meaningful to me. First of all if it has a positive impact on the environment in the wider sense, has a positive impact on people, on what they do, on how they are treated, the way business is being done, how people relate to each other, anything along those lines. Meaning is also, in a sense, about me getting personal satisfaction from what I do. Overall, I feel that my current work provides me that sense of meaning. Sometimes it is hard to remind me of that when I am doing a lot of detailed work. When I take a different perspective and see the wider picture, I get that sense of meaning. I had that sense of meaning very much at the beginning, for the first three years of my time working here, since I kind of lost the bigger picture perspective, which I think I regained recently. Could there be more, yes, and that's exactly what I said earlier, there are areas we are not tapping in yet. It is to be seen whether we are ever going to be tapping into these areas but I think there is a space for that. I think we need to think about the future too and that is what I am trying to get at: could there be a different economy? Yes, there could be. Could there be a different way of doing business and redefining business objectives? I believe yes. The bottom line is not just about shareholder value. Can the 'triple bottom line' be brought back to the top of the agenda? I believe so. There are different types of organisations, there are non-for-profit organisations, social businesses, all those sort of organisations operating on different value systems, different objectives, aiming at having a positive impact on society and the world at large. Some organisations cannot afford the type of services we offer, some do not even think about it, but they can gain massively from it. I think there is a whole area that is totally untapped. That for me, is an area we could further explore that would be fully aligned with my perspective, that I would be looking for and gain a massive satisfaction from, fulfilling that thirst for meaning. Today, when you get the basics covered, a lot of people are talking about having meaning in what they do on a daily basis.

Interviewer: Would you expect your organisation to do and explore that opportunity for you or would you consider proactively making things happen.

JF: Well, it can be and should be both. I don't want to having to push constantly, and it all depends if my push ends up becoming concrete and transforms into action or not. I would like to see an organisation having that vision that is already kind of there. We can help them define that vision more clearly and work towards achieving that vision but it cannot all be coming from employees. The organisation I believe should be laying out this vision and engaging employees with that vision.

Meaning is an interesting topic that I have come to think about more and more. A lot of it is in dialogue with other people, people looking for meaning in their work. Most of the time I find that the notion of meaning is linked to a potential positive contribution to the environment, to society, where they would like to see a positive impact on what it is that they do. Creativity is another subtheme, having freedom to apply new ways of doing things, doing things slightly differently, the ability to fulfil your potential, and related to a positive outcome, with an intrinsic satisfaction rather than just having a job that pays well. There are probably more and more young people, people who have been in their jobs for a while, who maybe got lured into supposedly attractive jobs, that on the outset sounded very sexy, let's say consultancy or the financial world, where you get a sniff of the glamour, of boardrooms and flying business class. However, after a while they realise it is a trap of political agendas, long hours that you often don't get satisfaction from. If you are lucky, the money is good but does that really make up for the quality, or rather lack of quality of life? And then I presume comes a moment of crisis where you go 'is that really what life is all about?' Since we spend so much time at work, work becomes our life and you start thinking, 'is that really what I was looking for in my life?'. Ultimately, you've got to start thinking of the meaning of what you are doing.

Interviewer: So do you think drivers change over time?

JF: Yes, I do think they change over time. It is always the relationship between expectations and reality and it depends on how much those two diverge, the gap between the two. If you have expectations that are being met, that's great. If they are not, then that's a completely different story. These may change over time. At the beginning for me, human processes, knowledge processes in organisations were at the core of what I wanted to do, but this has slightly changed. I see a bigger picture now, I see an interconnected macrocosm where we have individuals, groups, societies, countries, regions, organisations, we have cultures, the environment, nature, a lot of things and they are all interrelated and have an impact on each other. We need to think about how those can all impact each other in a way that is not harmful. So, yes as an individual, this has shifted over time. Some aspects have stayed the same, some others have widened as I started changing my perspective.

Interviewer: Now, if we think about the second notion Patrizia touched upon, the one of 'magic', how would you define that, what does that mean for you?

JF: Magic, I have mixed feelings about this one. Magic to me is when you have that feeling of 'above', you know, of excitement in a way and that, I believe, can be related to a whole range of things. There are moments at work when, let's say, you go travelling and have a meeting with the executive of an organisation, you had a great presentation and you felt you got a message across, people are getting the message, you have great and exciting moments there. In that room at that moment, the energy is magic to me. At the same time, magic is also something that you feel when you are achieving something meaningful. As I said before, this would have to go beyond my current work and engaging executives to talk about their people, it would have to be something greater than that. There are different themes that interconnect and if you can broaden that conversation and its impact that would feel more magical to me. I feel the notion of magic is something pretty unsustainable over time; it is not something you can have on a constant basis. There are always going to be brief moments of magic. It is a little bit like happiness: on the long term, it is neither achievable nor realistic and I am not sure this is something that you should be looking for constantly. It is good to experience it once in a while but something like meaning appears to me more sustainable over time, if you are able to create that meaning in your life through a job. And that is a totally different conversation but the question then is whether your job is there to provide meaning to your life or are there other things? Should they be mutually exclusive? Should they be the same thing? That is up to the individual to decide if they are happy with a 'meaningless' job and searching meaning elsewhere or has everything got to be collapsing under one big umbrella that is your job? We talk about work/life balance. Is there a balance? Does there need to be a balance?

Interviewer: Have you ever personally felt some magic in your work?

JF: Yes. Everything that is new and exciting is always magic. So when you start a job, if you have new experiences, a certain interest in your work where there is excitement, meeting new people, travelling, having energy in a room. That's magic and yes, I have experienced that. When I talk about a dynamic in the room, it is not only meetings with clients but also the dynamic you have with your colleagues, when you have a special bond, a great level of connection, exchanges of ideas and conversations.

I have to make this point: when I asked earlier if meaning should be connected to the job or not, some people have different perspectives. Some argue that artists have a magical job as well as meaning, that they are able to express who they are every day. It is quite different to working on an assembly line every day and repeating the same task over and over again. Is that magic and can it ever be achieved? I think you can always find some meaning in your work but if it is hard to find for you, I would like to see a model in the future where all of us can be part of society in a way that enables us to work, maybe a couple of days a week, or one day a week maybe, for the community. We could all be part of a charity and in agreement with your employer; you will be doing different jobs during the week. We could develop a more flexible model I guess: one where you are being paid, one where you do voluntary work. If everyone would do that, it may bring some more meaning and magic as well.

Magic to me is also highly linked to creativity and the ability to express yourself. We all have some degree of creativity but it is difficult to find the space to express it. It is down to all of us to use it in your own time but in addition to that, I would like to bring more of that into the daily routine at work, to have more space for creativity. Taking some time to think about the way we do work, rethinking how we work and relate to each other. Organisations today are very much outside of society, although also very much part of it, but we should take time to rethink the whole model of work and have that connected to the rest of society: have one voluntary job where you contribute to society and community and one where you do paid work. But they should not be so separate, that should just be the way we do things. Our company today gives us one day a year for voluntary work and no one uses it, but I think that's because one day is ridiculous. If I saw this as having a big impact and being taken seriously that would be different. If I was working four days a week for my company and one day doing something completely different, which would also benefit me as an individual and have a continuous impact on something, it would be a different story. As an individual, you can only grow from such an experience, which, obviously, you are going to bring back to the organisation. If you want to talk about balancing the different aspects of your life, that would help to gain exposure to different types of environments, which is more exciting.

Interviewer: OK. And what about money?

JF: In the hierarchy, if I had to choose between magic and money, even though I have to put a caveat around the notion of magic because I don't think it is sustainable overtime, it would be magic over money, that is for sure. But still, you need to be able to pay your bills as well as having a little bit extra. It is important to get your basics and needs covered, a little bit of your wants as well. If I had the choice to take a highly paid job with no meaning nor magic, I would not go for that. For me, meaning is first, it is all about the content of my work, which has several aspects: what is my impact, what is the bottom line, what do I achieve for myself and the people I work with; but also, the actual content of my work, what is it that I am doing on a daily basis. There are some tasks that appear more meaningful, but again, that term is quite stretchable since some might be quite meaningful but actually boring. Money comes after. I do not really want to include magic here because I think if you have meaning in your job, this will bring magic from time to time. If you have the luxury to choose your job and your career, that is a very important point. You can always argue what is the purpose of life but if you have the luxury to define that and make it for yourself, that's great, but not many people are in that position.

Interviewer: Considering you have been with your organisation for a while now, about 6 years, is that an indication that you have found the right balance between meaning, and money?

JF: Hmm. Not sure yet. I have learnt a lot, I have evolved, changed, but it is still to be seen. It is the longest time I have spent in any place but I am lacking comparisons there. 20 years from now, looking back I would probably look at it completely differently. It is hard to say. Right now, yes, there is balance. Can that be stretched and improved? Yes, absolutely. I like to be challenged and do different things at the same time. I would like to see more creativity in my work. I like to work in a place that is fast paced and global, challenging in many different ways such as where I work now, but there are other aspects that I would like to do more of that I am not currently doing.

Interviewer: It is interesting you have not yet mentioned anything around your research and the fact that you engaged a few years back in a part-time PhD. How does that tie in?

JF: I have learnt something very important during my PhD and that is the notion of identity. I have come to question the notion of identity more and more and how important it is. For me, personally, it is very important: how do I see my identity. We all have different identities but a big part of it is our job. Typically, in a social gathering, the first question people ask is 'what do you do'? For me, it is always a little more complicated to explain what I do. If you are an architect, people do not question what that is because they understand roughly what it is: you design buildings and places. It is more difficult for me I guess. For me, coming from Germany, the notion of work has a particular weight, we call it 'Beruf', which means 'what you have been called to do', 'your destiny'; so since I did my undergraduate in psychology, I have defined myself and thought of myself as a psychologist, an organisational psychologist. I was trying to further manifest that identity, and actually cementing that identity more and more, I wanted to be even more of a qualified psychologist. That is not the only reason why I have started a PhD. It is important for me to be a specialist in that field and opening up different avenues. But it is very close to the aspect of identity. Over the years, I have reached the conclusion that it is probably too narrow of a definition for myself. I am more than how I try to define myself or force myself into. There are several aspects. I always want to see it broader and not limited to that particular category.

Artists are exceptions of course but I like looking at this and how their identity is completely entangled into what they are doing. They are completely living their art. It defines who they are and their art is an expression of their inner self, emotions, and thoughts. I would say that this is an ideal state of being. I know this may be dangerous and that we talked about work/life balance but interestingly, we talk about balance distinguishing between the two, keeping them separate. Whereas I believe, the more they are in balance, the more they are in harmony. Do I have a balance? Do I need one? Does work have to provide all the meaning in my live? I am still searching for the answers and it is all in development of course. At the moment, the boundaries between work and life are not clearly defined, if you think about working at week-ends, responding to emails late at night, that is clearly not in balance but it is difficult to define what that balance means. If an artist gets a burst of creativity at ten in the evening, he is not going to think that this is an intrusion into his private life. He is always working, or not working, it is more up to his creativity. It depends on how you look at the notion of work. It also depends on the meaning you see, the motivation you have for your job. Some people see work as a way to get a salary, some do not. The more you perceive it as a pain, the more you want a balance. The more you are aligned with your work, the less you feel the need for that balance because you are truly passionate and enjoy what you do. For me, today, it depends. I always want to do a good job. Last night for example, I picked up the phone and had a conversation with my client at a time many would see way passed their normal working hours, and sent a few emails because I knew today was an important day for them. I wanted to be there and support. It does not bother me because it is important to me. There are other times when there are tasks where you think you have other things in your life that are more important and where it feels more intruding into your private sphere. There are times when you do not want to deal with them. There is no answer to this, there is no balance really, it depends on the time, the circumstances, the people involved, the task at hand. I am using the word 'balance' even though I don't like it. It is not the right word to describe it.

Interviewer: Before we started, you said you would have liked not to have read the narrative and start this conversation fresh. Why is that?

JF: Well, Patrizia's narrative is in chronological order; university, then her consulting job then she discussed where she is today, and it feels as if life has gone a full circle in a way. She is comparing before and after in a way, and is now in a positive situation. Looking back she has a real possibility to analyse that from an observer's perspective. I found that perspective very interesting. At the time she might not have seen all those things because she did not have the time to think or breath. All these phenomena she describes, and using academic quotes, I was thinking that I have not done that level of in-depth analysis of work. I was wondering if you were expecting me to have done that analysis for our chat today but then I realized that that was different, that it is about my experience, which is different.

The way she describes management consultancy, I must admit, I am quite glad I am not working there. As I said at the beginning, I did not want to be part of the traditional management consulting job. We learnt at university a little bit about what that world might be like and I knew I did not want to be part of this. Even though she describes how people are supporting each other because it is in the 'DNA', it sounds like a good spirit but I think it is there for the wrong reasons. It is 'either up or out', which is not part of our culture here at all. We always had a more collaborative spirit, because we wanted to and because we had a great team spirit, a natural dynamic that was there in the first place, not because we had to in order to survive. Her world was a lot more hostile than the world I am in, and yet, we are working long hours, on average maybe more than others but it is still manageable and it feels that there is sometimes still some breathing space. You know, giving people a company car at the beginning, they are creating this image of a glamorous world, which, from the inside, is not glamorous at all, all you are doing is delivering PowerPoint presentations and doing analysis for more senior consultants. You are just doing the leg work. Some people are happy with that, and happy to define their identity this way, having the big car, the money, the technology and all of that. In that respect, coming back to the meaning aspect, this is not how I see myself; this is not what motivates me. To identify myself with the role of a consultant, I can absolutely do that, but only if it comes with meaningful relationships and conversations, to become a trusted advisor. In principle, that is an identity I can relate to very much when it has a certain level of depth, and especially when the relationships develop over time.

Interviewer: What about the future? If you were to project yourself in an ideal situation, work-wise, how would that look like?

JF: I have changed over time and went into different directions, I have many different interests. So for me, a good future would enable me to do more of the things that I like. This comes back to what I was saying originally, if I could work three days a week as a consultant, one day doing something charitable and one day doing something more artistic maybe, that would be ideal. It would be a great balance for me overall. Just doing one of them in itself would not be enough for me, it would have to be the combination that I would enjoy doing.

In an ideal world, I believe work should be as close as possible to who we are as a person, it should be fulfilling, it should be meaningful, whatever that might mean to the individual. Work should make use as much as possible of your skills and talents, have the meaning you are looking for in life, and hopefully, have a positive impact on the wider environment.

Interviewer: I think this sums it up nicely. Thank you Johannes

PART 2:

Mapping the Territory

Mapping the Territory

Eidi Cruz-Valdivieso

"The map is not the territory"
Alfred Korzybski[18]

A few words on Eidi

Eidi was born in Mexico City where she worked for many years amongst some of the poorest communities in the areas of co-creativity, mentorship and community integration. She studied psychology in Mexico, and later studied organisational and social psychology and worked at the London School of Economics looking at intellectual capital in five European countries in a joint project with the European Commission; and at co-creation in the marketing industry. During the years she lived in London also studied acting. Her passion is for social transformation, art and creativity to find a common platform, which can encourage others to create new possibilities, expressed in tangible actions. Currently she is leading a programme that promotes creativity and innovation by incentivizing some of the best social entrepreneurs and innovators around the world.

---

[18] Korzybski, A. (1933). A Non-Aristotelian System and its Necessity for Rigour in Mathematics and Physics. Science and Sanity

A new route...

Around 4 years ago my family and I were in a restaurant with a family friend, a wonderful British photographer, who had come to Mexico to shoot a series of pictures of my parents' organisation in order to write a book with them. We were all at the table waiting for our food to arrive when he innocently asked my brother and I, 'What is the most amazing story that you experienced with your parents living in these communities?' After a few seconds my brother replied, 'there are some images that started coming to my mind as we went into the first community today and heard our parents tell you about the beginning of their work, but they are a bit hazy. See if you can remember Eidi.' My brother started describing the images of being in a car and stuck in what we thought was traffic. I was 11 and he was 6. There was blood and a wounded guy that ended up in the car with us. As my brother continued describing the images, I started joining in and finishing his sentences. A gang fight, our mother recognising a young man who had been shot and stopping the car to go down and help him, telling us from the window 'Whatever happens, don't step out of the car!'. A few moments later this young guy, who had just been shot was in the car with us. My mother starts driving again and we go through the traffic into the main roads of the city to find a hospital.

For obvious reasons my brother and I had blocked this from our day-to-day memory, and so, as we finished remembering, my mother retold the story. The teenager who had been shot in a gang fight in front of us was only seventeen and we knew his mother and siblings, and there was no way my mother was going to leave him in the streets bleeding after he had been shot.

What is work? As a child I had the opportunity to see the creation of work, rather than the finding of it. When my brother and I were children, my parents created an organisation to work alongside some of the poorest communities in Mexico. This work started in Oaxaca City in the south of Mexico, where we lived for two years, and later continued in Mexico City. My father had enjoyed every academic success and was continuing his promising career in the pharmaceutical industry as a business strategist. My mother also had a bright professional future in front of her after studying medicine. However, after a few years, because of their convictions, my parents decided to start working in the poorest area of Mexico City, which meant a radical change in our family lifestyle. My father's vision was to create an urban transformation centre, in order to provide the communities a learning platform that was truly local and contextual, shaped by the community members and which could allow them to create systems to help themselves. The first community centre was built in an area of open sewage canals and little shacks built over piles of rubbish, in an area that was originally mined to build the main roads of the now 23 plus million people in Mexico City. A space was created for initiative, integration, encouragement, empowerment and education, where the communities could learn to collaborate and transform their situation into new possibilities for themselves and their community.

From the beginning my brother and I were involved in the work. We would follow our parents into the shanty-town communities so we would learn alongside them and get to know the people who lived there. We would go to 'work' (play) with the children in the community, eat with them, learn with and from them. We would hear our parents motivate with words and actions hundreds of people that would start seeing their possibilities in a different light and learn new ways of thinking and acting on their situation. Through understanding their love and passion for this work, we also fell in love with these communities and this work became our family work and organisation. I saw the constant creation of new projects that originated infrastructure, jobs, relationships and more possibilities for the communities. With the ups and downs that any entrepreneurial endeavour implies, I saw an organisation grow, set up more community centres and projects. I saw women setting up systems that would look after and improve nutrition for their children. I saw adults that had left school at an early age start studying again. Several other small – what we now call social – enterprises were started. There were over 80 houses built, in an area which had previously been mined - which required a lighter building material to be used, and I saw the creation of rice husk panels, a new technology co-engineered by the community, an architect and my father, which were weather insulating and fire retardant. As I grew up and I started working more formally with them I got involved in urban and rural projects of community integration, leadership, education and art. We travelled for many years to the mountains in Oaxaca and created a platform so that the indigenous students in this region could go through high school and university. These students were and are the first generation in their family, and many times in their village, to go through high school and university.

Those living in these deprived areas, and the hundreds of volunteers from around the world who visited and lived with us, all became our friends and our extended family. We all experienced the creation of a very heterogeneous community that loved working and creating together.

The territory as context

I was living in London at the time of the global financial crisis. I had just graduated from a Master's degree in Organisational and Social Psychology at the LSE and had immediately started working at this university as a research officer in a project funded by the European Commission, promoting collaboration and strengthening competitiveness and the innovation capabilities of small and medium enterprises in Europe, and implementing a program for Intellectual Capital and Collaboration. The time of the financial crisis was a time to reset priorities for many. Collaboration was an approach that seemed appropriate and which created virtuous cycles. In my experience, the idea and practice of collaboration and co-creation in the different areas of this work, promoted creativity through allowing more complex processes find new solution paths. Collaboration also provided a space to remain global and local, respecting and enhancing the different contexts from where people and companies were coming from.

At that time, being in an academic context, conversations with friends oscillated between two main possibilities: if the financial situation and career prospects were not promising, people were asking themselves what was it that they really wanted to do beyond what they were supposed to do with/for their career; secondly, if the financial situation and career prospects were still promising, what could we create that would not only develop our career path but would benefit others and somehow respond to the problems that this crisis was deepening. New possibilities were emerging.

We were privileged to have the time to have the conversations about these matters with people from so many different backgrounds and nationalities and therefore to explore these ideas from many angles. Most of us who graduated from this MSc had also worked for a few years before we started this course and so these conversations were highly enriched by the work experiences we already had.

Since part of my context was (and is) also Mexico and Latin America, it is important to mention the impact that the global financial crisis had in the region. At the time of the financial downturn things were unfortunately getting worse in our countries due to the already damaged economy, corruption and years of consequences: the lack of virtuous national systems, of education, of work opportunities, etc.

In 2009 severe collateral damages to our economy could be seen due to the impact of the global downturn (Aguilera and Rossi, 2009)[19]. Although, this took place after the longest period of sustained growth since the 1970s, which had left previously crisis-prone countries with stronger economies than before, to some, the financial forecasts made by the major international institutions were underestimating the scale of the local crisis in 2009. Even more alarming was the social repercussions which can be more severe and prolonged than the slowdown in economic growth. 'Although it is too early to fully assess the impacts of the crisis on indicators such as poverty, inequality and employment, the global

[19] Aguilera, R. & Rossi, V. (2009). From Steady Growth to Sudden Crisis: How Latin America and the Caribbean are Coping with the Global Recession. International Economics Working Paper, IEP WP (09/01)

recession is expected to reverse many of the social gains realised during the growth period [...]'. (Aguilera and Rossi, 2009)[20].

Looking slightly further back: after the North American Free Trade Agreement (NAFTA) was signed in 1992 and came into force in January 1994 – although many in Mexico started to build their hopes and the core of their career ambitions around the transnational corporations that arrived in the country with this trade agreement – it was clear that those at the bottom of the pyramid would very seldom see the benefits of this agreement. Education didn't improve, nor did employment opportunities for the marginalised communities; and in the midst of some being captivated by the promise of a new corporate land, a very serious devaluation was building up. In January 1994 we saw the emergence of the Ejército Zapatista de Liberación Nacional (EZLN), better known as the Zapatistas; and the murder of one of the presidential candidates in March that same year, creating a completely new scenario for the country and those of us growing up at the time.

These years in Mexican history should be explored further, but for now, let's say that this was a very important part of our context growing up. Decisions regarding careers were made several years later, but there were substantial mental notes that had been made. I believe that there was a subtle, yet important, division that these years created on our social involvement perspective. Many took the stance that since they were living in such a conflicted country, staying away from holding strong political, social and economic

---

[20] Aguilera, R. & Rossi, V. (2009). From Steady Growth to Sudden Crisis: How Latin America and the Caribbean are Coping with the Global Recession. International Economics Working Paper, IEP WP (09/01)

views (i.e. talking about them, having any kind of informed opinion or participating in any way) would keep them safe from its consequences, which were only perpetuated by the lack of a stronger generational voice being shaped. Many others, however, decided to get involved in the reality of our cities.

I came back to Mexico over two years ago and started working for a non-profit, leading a program that incentivises some of the most impressive high impact social entrepreneurs and innovators around the world. I believe that creativity and innovation have started to flourish even further in this area. For the last several years the social entrepreneurship ecosystem in Latin America, and globally, is rapidly growing, and the technologies that are being developed are fostering an exponential growth that is evidently changing our reality at an accelerated pace. Nearly seven years after the global financial crisis we see more and more evidence of the decisions that were taken at that time, choices that did not only respond to the belief that having a career is only to satisfy our personal needs and interests, but that responded to a reality in our own contexts and made us more reflective over the privileged situation in which we are in.

Alignment

As we explore work, we think immediately of the role that this plays in our life and our fulfilment, and raise questions regarding our experience of it, and if this process is actually taking us to where we envisioned our life would go to, if in fact we are going in the direction of fulfilling our life expectations and adding value. Given my upbringing and the different contexts in which I was raised, lived and worked, I believe that in order to go through a fulfilling working life we need to look at three different areas regarding work and use our creativity to promote the intersection between them - to find their alignment. For me these areas are: what we love to do, what we are good at doing, and what needs to be done. The alignment of these areas helps us create a vision not only for our working lives but for our lives in general. The alignment between what we love to do — our passions and our dreams; what we are good at doing — our talents, abilities, skills and expertise in the context of a real level of challenge when performing these; and what needs to be done — the critical needs on our local and global contexts, can allow us create new possibilities not only for us but for others around us as well.

Let me explain what I mean with these three areas, and support this through the approaches of two different writers:

What we love to do can be a wonderful area of exploration. To give our passions and dreams the importance that they deserve is a freeing and I feel, an important exercise, not only for us as individuals, but for society. With passion I mean the area of life, and in this particular case, working life, that makes us lose track of time and that engages us completely. For some this can be as easy as to know that they are captivated by dance, by music, by mathematics, by biology, by a particular sport, etc. For others it might not be such an obvious encounter, but it can certainly be found if exploring for it with a certain degree of diligence. This area is what Sir Ken Robinson has called our element (2009)[21]. With dreams I mean how we envision ourselves practicing, working and

[21] Robinson, K. (2009). The Element: How Finding Your Passion Changes Everything. New York: Penguin Books.

succeeding in the particular areas of work that we find the most engaging, and the factors that need to be part of the equation in order for this to be fulfilling and add value.

What we are good at, and the practice of this, has an important impact on how we feel about our day to day experience of work. The level of satisfaction that we have from the activities we perform everyday influences our overall sense of well-being. I have learned much more about this through the work of Mihály Csíkszentmihályi (1990)[22]. He describes this as the finding of flow, and the optimal experience, and explains specific conditions that can be promoted by everyone. He says that in order to find flow we need: clear goals, immediate feedback and a balance between opportunity and capacity. This feeling of flow then takes place when challenges and skills are high and equal to each other, and concentration on the task deepens as the task at hand demands complete attention (Csíkszentmihályi, 2003)[23]. With this I'm not trying to present a specific approach as the answer, but rather highlight a methodology that has at its core the promotion of well-being in the context of work, characterised by elements such as: achievement, endurance, cognitive structure, order, play, and low impulsivity, all of them crucial for the life of organisations and its employees.

There is a pause to make regarding the last area of these three: what needs to be done, as we are all aware of the state of things around us, the critical needs that many people have in our surroundings, or even far away, and the systemic impact that this

---

[22] Csikszentmihalyi, M. (1990). Flow: The Psychology of Optimal Experience. New York: Harper & Row

[23] Csikszentmihalyi, Mihaly (2003). Good Business: Leadership, Flow, and the Making of Meaning. New York: Basic Books.

also has on us all. What needs to be done could, however, be interpreted in two ways: an imposition – having to do something that we could see as an option or somebody else's responsibility (i.e. the government, the NGOs, etc.) – or we could see it as an invitation to engage in a creative way from our own platform, or own reality and using our own passions and abilities, talents and skills. In other words I believe that there is so much to be done, that we could creatively try to participate in one way or another and that this participation does not depend on our level of altruism, our financial possibilities or the amount of time that we have to spare, but rather in our openness to care about it and creatively act upon this, in one way or another.

Beyond what we used to call work-life balance, we now think in terms of finding meaning and fulfilment as a generation and being able to add value. And so, this is more than a desire to find balance, it is an exercise that requires discipline and intentionality. However, our intentionality commonly leads us to think that we need to focus mainly on our own safety, happiness, pleasure, progress, and that this would ultimately bring fulfilment. However, many theorists have stated that work is in fact what brings a very important proportion of our life fulfilment, and interestingly, many of the studies and research on what makes people happy also found that it has to do with being generous with others, whether as an act of kindness (Achor, 2011)[24], the nurturing of relationships, or the ability to focus more on the exterior rather than ourselves (Schwartz, 2009)[25], happiness and fulfilment continuously bring us

---

[24] Achor, S. (2011). The happy secret to better work. [Video]. Retrieved from https://www.ted.com/talks/shawn_achor_the_happy_secret_to_better_work

[25] Schwartz, B. (2009). Our Loss of Wisdom. [Video]. Retrieved from http://www.ted.com/talks/barry_schwartz_on_our_loss_of_wisdom

back to the need to be aware of our context as a constant deliberate action. Through Csíkszentmihályi's years of research about finding flow we learn that as part of the results of studying very successful CEOs he found out that 'These people define success as something that helps others and at the same time makes [them] you feel happy as [they] you are working at it…' (2003)[26].

My own route and the case of creativity

I believe that in order to find alignment between the three areas that I previously mentioned, we need to deliberately exercise creativity. Through exercising our creativity we can generate a vision, and as we embrace this vision we could then understand our perspective on leadership and develop it.

For many years I have been profoundly interested in the importance of the deliberate exercise of creativity, partly for my love of the performing arts and partly because of my psychology background. When I was studying psychology at university some teachers would look at me with disapproval and would challenge why I was not looking at the 'real things', the 'real problems and solutions' and write essays about pathology and disorders instead of creativity and artistic processes. My main problem with those 'real problems and solutions' was that it was difficult to spend my time making the most of all the knowledge that had already been standardised in one culture and arbitrarily used in every other! Later, however, through my father, I met a wonderful group of

---

[26] Csikszentmihalyi, Mihaly (2003). Good Business: Leadership, Flow, and the Making of Meaning. New York: Basic Books.

psychologists who were exploring collaborative, positive and narrative approaches to therapy, and I studied and worked with these new tools for a few years. These new approaches strengthened my love for the creative processes and my interest in collaboration, which although I have seldom mentioned in this narrative, it has been expressed in my love for integration of heterogeneous communities and the ability that we have to co-create.

As we look at the impact that the global financial crisis had in our generation, in the context of work, I think we can safely say that we can see a growth in entrepreneurship and innovation, even an exponential growth in some cases. These entrepreneurs and innovators are aligning their priorities and exercising creativity as core elements of their working life. During one of the LSE lectures at the start of the financial crisis in 2008, Lord Meghnad Desai said 'You are a lucky generation because you have lived through one of the great crashes of capitalism' (2008)[27].

Several years after, we can hear in the voice of Matthew Taylor, Chief Executive of the RSA, that 'it can be retrospectively clear that, during some of the gloomiest periods in history there has also been a rise in the amount of innovation' (2014)[28]. We can see that part of the aftermath of the global financial crisis has been in fact more entrepreneurship, more innovation, and although we need to balance a positive side of this with a fair analysis of whether this

---

[27] Desai, M. (2008). The Great Crash of 2008: Causes, Consequences and the Future of the World Economic System [Audio]. Retrieved from http://www.lse.ac.uk/study/summerSchools/summerSchool/About_LSE_SummerSchool/The-Great-Crash-of-2008-Causes,-Consequences-and-the-Future-of-the-World-Economic-System.aspx

[28] Taylor, M. (2014). The Power to Create. RSA Chief Executive's lecture. [Video]. Retrieved from https://www.thersa.org/discover/videos/event-videos/2014/07/power-to-create/

creates or strengthens a more or a less stable economy, during a panel held at the RSA, experts were asking the following: 'Will the entrepreneurial drive of the Millennial generation shape the zeitgeist for the first half of 21st century, harnessing transformations in the way we live and work to drive up productivity and living standards?' (Taylor et al., 2014)[29].

Looking at the abundance of projects that have been developed since those nearly seven years ago, and seeing how many have been successful, I do believe that there is a space for the exercise and implementation of creative ideas that is allowing faster and more surprising change. Without trying to be over optimistic, I do believe that technology has enhanced our entrepreneurial platform and that this is allowing even more creativity to flow. Those that are heading the institutions that promote creativity, innovation, art, enterprising, etc., know that we are witnessing a time in which not only the elite have the possibility to exercise creativity, but that 'an unprecedented opportunity - powerful social and technological change, which means that we can now realistically commit to the aspiration that every citizen should have a creative life.' (Taylor et al., 2014)[29].

The accelerated technological and social changes during the last few years: the ability we have to be instantaneously connected, autonomy in communications (to a greater or lesser degree), and our immediate notion of other's realities is opening more than ever, a space for the creation of new scenarios. H. G. Wells wrote in 1902: 'In the past century, there were more changes than in the previous thousand years. The new century will see changes that

[29] Taylor, M., Fox, M.L., Howker, E., Pirie, M., & Lent, A. (2012, September). The Millennials Debate. [Video]. Retrieved from: https://www.thersa.org/events/2012/09/the-millennials-debate/

will dwarf those of the last'[30]. This has certainly proved to be the case and the pace of change is increasing. As Ray Kurzweil observes: 'An analysis of the history of technology shows that technological change is exponential, contrary to the common-sense 'intuitive linear' view. So we won't experience 100 years of progress in the 21st century - it will be more like 20,000 years of progress (at today's rate)' (2001)[31].

We can see this through a myriad of examples, showing how, because of the risks that have been taken in the past decade, there is an increasingly high number of new scenarios being created, that are finding alignment. In the work I currently do, which incentivises some of the best social entrepreneurs from around the world, I get to know every day yet one more initiative that was started in a different part of the world by a Millennial. The civil society and those that were taking career decisions at the time of the financial crisis seem to have taken the creation of new paths in their stride.

Part of my experience of work has been entrepreneurial and intra-preneurial. Mainly the latter, in the sense that I have worked for organisations that have allowed me to be creative and explore new territories in order to bring new results back. In this scenarios I have been able many times to be my own boss, lead others and define the new routes that we would take in order to bring new possibilities and even new platforms from where to expand the impact of the vision. I have really enjoyed and appreciated the possibility of growing the areas of my work and the inclusiveness

---

[30] Wells, H.G. (1902). Discovery of the Future. London: Royal Institution lecture quoted in Rees, M. (2004). Our Final Hour: A Scientist's Warning. New York: Basic Books.

[31] Kurzweil, R. (2001). The Law of Accelerating Returns. Retrieved from http://www.kurzweilai.net/the-law-of-accelerating-returns

that this has allowed me to have. This brings me back to the importance of vision and leadership.

A vision that is shaped by aligning our passion, our abilities and our context seems a good place to start, in order to give ourselves the flexibility of going through new paths creatively. Whatever our choice of sector and field of work is, and whatever the intrinsic motivations that we have to develop our selves professionally in them are, creating a vision allows the intentionality of our work to continue and the creativity to flow.

The advantage of a clear vision is that it provides a clear direction yet it allows us to explore new territories. I saw a lot of strength through the clarity of the vision that my parents had when they committed to working with some of the poorest communities in the country, and this clarity allowed them to have a very tangible sense of leadership that made them and their work very compelling. Their vision continued to be shaped through time, but it was very strong from the beginning because it was very defined and it was originated from a place of integrity and creativity. They wanted to learn to work with extremely impoverished communities, and together with them create new platforms that would allow these children, youth and adults to find solutions to their own problems, create virtuous systems around their needs and be creative to generate opportunities for infrastructure, integration, health, education and art, not only for the individuals but for the communities as well. Their type of leadership had two elements that I have very rarely seen in other organisations. They wanted to walk alongside the people that they were leading, as they understood that leadership was also a way of teaching others how to have agency of their own process; and therefore, they promoted local leadership and initiative as two of the core principles of their organisation.

Generally, in my experience of work, I have continued to see the fundamental impact that vision and leadership have when they are truly present. When I or others allow an exploration of new creative routes to find alignment by being loyal to our passions and dreams, being devoted to learning and growing in expertise, skills and ability in a particular area, and committing to look beyond ourselves, and therefore include our contexts (and others' well-being as well as ours) into our life path. This promotes clarity, an opportunity to generate a vision around the 'what', which helps us to be more flexible around the 'how to's'.

Most of my work has had a strong element of collaboration, and in my experience, this is an area that although can be challenging, sets a platform to integrate the different areas of our life and enhances their alignment. When we work collaboratively and interdisciplinary, the different angles through which we see the needs, the solutions and the growth of the work we do, does not only allow our perspective to become richer, but also creates a more complex process which, in order to be solved, requires new creative paths. It would seem that in our globalised context to be collaborative is a necessity rather than an option, as we constantly need to integrate the different perspectives and voices of others, in order to be relevant and find harmony in our work.

To conclude: Exploring new routes

The idea of context has been very important throughout my life, the appreciation of our reality beyond what we can do for ourselves and our closest ones, was the way I learned through which to shape a career path whatever our choice of field was. Looking at our context requires us to take a stance about what to do about it when we give it an honest look. It all starts there, the perspective that we have about our level of engagement with the reality of others, and not only ours can be a crucial element of the direction of where we are heading. This, I believe is an on-going process, as the different moments in our lives, our passions, interest and dreams continue to be shaped throughout it, and so we need to have a constant process of re-invention between what we want to do, what we are good at doing, and what needs to be done. 'We have been brought up with this idea that life is linear... when in fact we can create and re-create our life' (Robinson, 2009)[32].

The idea of a territory being different to the map fascinates me on several levels, and I found at least two pertinent reasons to mention it in this narrative. The first one has to do with language and this is in fact the direction in which the phrase by Alfred Korzybski 'The map is not the territory' (1933)[33] was originally coined. If our human knowledge is limited by the languages that we have developed (general semantics), and therefore our experience of reality is filtered through the brain's responses to it (Korzybski, 1933)[33], how can we then expand the reach of our

---

[32] Robinson, K. (2006). How schools kill creativity. [Video]. Retrieved from https://www.ted.com/talks/ken_robinson_says_schools_kill_creativity

[33] Korzybski, A. (1933). A Non-Aristotelian System and its Necessity for Rigour in Mathematics and Physics. Science and Sanity

perspectives and create new possibilities? Simplistically speaking the extent of our vocabulary, the choice of phrases we live around and the ideas that have been constructed through these, forge our reality to a great extent. To me, we could therefore see that the integration of creativity and collaboration in our work life is key so we are constantly exploring new ways of thinking, solving, creating and growing. Secondly, through my upbringing I learned that work was an art and a joy, through which we could create new possibilities in order to explore new routes of working and living, and that through this freedom and privilege we could align our passions, our talents and our context in order to have a fulfilling and meaningful life and provide others with a better platform to achieve this as well. For me part of the art of living is to learn to integrate work into it, rather than compartmentalise it away from the rest of what we do. Finding that intersection between our work and our life, creating a multifaceted identity that gives us the versatility to make our intentions be constructed, rather than living to find a balance between work and life (or work and rest) seems to be a good start.

In terms of vision and leadership, the main type of leadership that I've learned from, was the one I saw from a very early age. It started with the creation of an inclusive and strong vision which set the foundations, for me and many others, to think creatively, and therefore freely about what work means; as well as committedly, and therefore integrally about our engagement with society.

It is important to say that, as a friend of mine put it, to participate socially and engage in others' problematic reality is not necessarily part of our DNA, but rather a constant decision that is made consciously and many times, lovingly. I believe that this engagement, and the alignment that I have been mentioning, is a lifelong process. As we go through life we are shaped and re-shaped and this has an impact on our priorities and interests; which ultimately has an impact on the alignment between what we love to do, what we are good at doing, and what needs to be done. I have decided for many years to prioritise my work in a few of the areas that I'm passionate about, however, there could be further alignment to make, which would allow me to integrate other areas too. I believe that as we go through our working life, we are all invited to create and re-create.

Discussing the narrative with Manuel Riveros

"The way I see it, career is a way of living. It is not something that you do"

A few words on Manuel

Manuel is a Chilean Business Consultant, an amateur Flamenco guitarist, a first-time marathoner and a happily married guy that loves a good glass of wine and a nice chat with friends. He is passionate about life and adding purpose to any project that he decide to embrace.

He studied Business Administration in Chile, a Master's degree in Organisational Psychology in London at the LSE, where he lived and worked for 5 years, and currently he is finishing a second one in Cultural-Biology back in his country where he currently lives. He has been working for the last 6 years at Pragmaxion, a consulting firm that brings complex initiatives to life, from building strategies with their clients, to enhancing collaboration and innovation with their partners.

Interview transcripts

Interviewer: To start with, can you please detail what you did after the LSE, what were your motivations at the time, and what you are doing now?

Manuel Riveros (MR): Well, after the LSE, I strayed another 2 years working for the European Union, with Professor Humphreys on a project called 'InCaS' – Intellectual Capital Statement. The idea was to develop 25 case studies on how to state intellectual capital in European small and medium sized enterprises (SMEs). I was doing this with Spanish SMEs, being based in London and travelling back and forth to Spain. And then I came back home, in Chile. I looked for a job for about six weeks. I did not know what to do. My main background is in Administration and Engineering, but before the LSE, I worked 5 years for a foundation that focused on developing entrepreneurship and leadership practices in Chile. During that experience, I learned a lot on the 'soft' stuff, things you typically develop while doing consulting: how to develop leaders, foster collaboration, help people work together, etc. Coming back, it was clear to me that I was not going to work in economics or engineering as would my previous classmates in Chile, I was not going to go to Finance, or RH.

Interviewer: Why do you say you 'knew' you would not go towards that direction?

MR: Because I see my career in a very flexible way. I see my parents' generation for example, they would say 'I am going to work for this bank for the next 30 years', at the end of which they may get a golden watch or any other object for their service. I have always felt that I wanted something different. When I say that with my career I am flexible, I mean that I want to be able to move around. It also means that I want flexibility in the way I work. I want to manage my own time, work from home if I need to – or on the beach or in the office as a matter of fact. I also want to be able to 'mix' my time: teach, as I work as a consultant, or doing other things such as research or studying. I am very keen on studying all the time. Currently, I am doing another Masters' degree in cultural biology.

The question of career is an interesting one. The way I see it, career is a way of living. It is not something that you do. I have never seen work as something that one does for a living, to pay your rent. For me that is where you put your passion! You just do something that is meaningful to you, as least for me. For example, when I was working for a foundation, I felt I was doing something that was useful to the country. Yes, I was developing skills for myself, but I was also doing something meaningful, and I put my heart into it! Everything I do now, even though I am working for a private consultancy, I think and live my work as doing something meaningful to Chile. In my day to day work, when I interact with people, I do work for them, and not just for the company they work for. That is why for me, it has been a way of living, not a way to pay the rent. When someone asks me: 'So, what do you do?', it is hard to say from my perspective. I am not what I study, I am half a consultant, half a researcher, probably a bit of a teacher and philosopher too.

Interviewer: If we think about it more practically, what do you actually do day to day?

MR: I am working for a Chilean private consulting organisation called Pragmaxion. I am a senior consultant, and a manager. I have been working here for the last four and a half years, almost five years, doing different kind of things, more aligned with what we would call 'soft skills'. Even if we have this 'soft' approach, we focus on developing processes, strategy and achieving business results. Even if we are engineers, we work with people.

Since I joined, I have been working mainly on 2 projects. The first one, for my initial two years here, I was working with the mining industry, developing suppliers' network and relationships within a 'win-win' environment for 250 SMEs. On one side, we worked with suppliers to help them develop their ways of working, their products and innovation skills. At the same time, we built the relationships within the miners themselves, and the partnership between miners and suppliers. We created the space so that relationship can emerge. We built innovation projects where both suppliers and miners were involved so that suppliers could, for instance, develop a new product fully adapted to the mining industry, and reach a 'win-win' result. For example, we designed better fitted tires for the mining trucks, adapted to the environment so they can actually last twice longer. The money that is then saved – in terms of not having to change tires as much – is split between the mining organisation and the supplier. That is just an example but there have been at least 25 projects such as this one being developed. What is great is that this collaboration space now exists. In the past, they hardly collaborated at all and hardly talked to one another. Putting things back into context, the mining industry in Chile is like going back to the 18th Century, which goes with a certain culture. The management culture is very old fashioned, patronising, leaders just ask for what they need and cut as much as they can. They cut on innovation, on collaboration and cut this space of 'new' and 'ifs', and any potential working space.

So basically, what we were doing was to build a new way of doing things. It had really incredible results in practice. The projects themselves were giving results, such as the example I gave you around tires. Tires lasted longer, so money was saved for miners and that meant that the supplier had a new product to offer to any other mine in the world. The collaborative and innovative space we created was completely new and other things started to develop as well, and new actors came onto the scene. At the start, there were miners and suppliers, but after a while, other miners wanted to participate and then the government, and then foundations, and now, there is a true cluster, which actually became the name of the project: the 'Chilean Cluster'. The idea of the cluster came from the Australian mining industry. Over there, the different actors in this industry live close to one another, suppliers close to miners, so the cluster is natural, it just happens, just like in the Silicon Valley. What we are doing artificially in Chile is to build a cluster which is not natural. It has been a very rich experience, new dynamics, new relationships, new products and services. In my role, I have been building these bridges, helping with strategies, with processes, providing new tools to elaborate offers and services. It was also important to build bridges between them and the government, foundations and banks.

So, I did this for two and a half years more or less. After that, I went to work in Lima, in Peru and applied the same idea. I worked there with Antamina, the second largest mining company in the world. They heard of our project and wanted to try it, in a Peruvian way, which is very different. Cultures are incredibly different. I was there for the first year and a half because we had no team in Peru. We started building the company's office over there. We had the excuse of this project, so it was easier. Today, there are five or six people working there and are still working on this project. I left last January, I could no longer keep on travelling, my wife was not really happy with me travelling every week, and for me it was very tiring as well, four hours each way, plus traffic and so on, it was horrible. It was a very tiring year and a half but I learnt a lot.

Now, I am doing OD – organisational development – with a team here in Chile with a huge company, building a team of about 30 people and we are developing that area. We are developing OD practices, leadership capabilities of the team in charge, various other things, new ways to collaborate, developing skills, doing workshops about what we do, it is a bit of everything.

Interviewer: One of the reasons we wanted to link Eidi's narrative with your interview was to discuss what you just mentioned around seeing work in a certain way, and also due to your connections to Latin America. One of the phrases Eidi refers to is *'the map is not the territory'*, and I am curious to hear from you what you read in that sentence and how does that resonate with you?

MR: To me, it comes back to what I said at the beginning, it is hard for me to say where I am going to be and what I will be doing in the next three to five years, and that is because I am really keen on keeping my 'flexibility' and the way my career is developing. I have seen around me that more and more people pay extreme attention to the way their careers develop. They are not particularly loyal to their companies anymore but rather to their own selves. This leads to a huge challenge for organisations. How does a company do to retain people happy and for longer? The way this idea of 'the territory and the map' resonates with me is that I believe there are no walls anymore. There are no limits anymore. Today I am in Chile but nothing prevents me from working in India tomorrow, or working on line. Who knows? We are not limited to the ground on which we are standing or to the company we are working for. The idea of 'flexibility' is that you do not attach your career to yourself. If you are a psychologist for example, you are no a psychologist 100% of your day and 24/7. I have made management studies, and economy, and biology but that does not mean I am a manager, an economist or a biologist. I am a bit of everything. It is very flexible, depending on the context I can switch hats and do different things.

Interviewer: Are you relating this to having different identities, several 'play grounds' for being yourself?

MR: I don't really mean we have different identities because for me, identity sounds fixed, and that you use the one more convenient for what you need at a particular time, and I don't think it is that way. I believe we are not really fixed any longer, but you have to go with the flow, learning as you go, on your way. You go and change along. We are not static anymore. I really believe that the career that you had before, where you started as a teacher for example and remained a teacher for your entire life does no longer exist. Now, you start with some initial education in an area but you know it does not define who you are. It is just a moment, but you keep on going, you are flexible. So, it is not different identities you can change when you want to, but you are changing on the way. You continue being 'one'.

Interviewer: Do you believe this comes more from a personal drive or rather from some external factors, and the simple fact that we don't really have a choice to change and adapt?

MR: Well, it is really complex. It is complicated to say that it is coming from one or the other. There are many reasons involved with what is going on. Probably we, as workers, professionals, are more aware of what we like and we try having fun. The idea of you waiting the end of your professional life to start having fun, rest and use your savings, buy a little house in the country side, is no longer a reality. We, as workers of this time, do want to have fun, do want to learn, do want to put our hearts in what we do, work passionately. We want to stand up and challenge things. We have the tools, and we are more aware of what we can do and we do really want to have fun. We want to enjoy what we do. But also, there are external elements such as globalisation. Today, around the world, many careers are flexible. At least, mine is. I don't know how flexible a doctor's career is. Maybe he works in an office, and then in a hospital, but clearly some careers are more flexible than others. In any case, globalisation is changing everything. If you don't do your work in a flexible way, someone in Finland, or India, or Japan will, and will work faster, better and cheaper. In a nutshell, it is not really an option. But that is not the only reason; most of us also want to have fun and enjoy what we do.

Interviewer: Eidi discusses the interplay between work and play, doing something that talks to your heart, and I do relate to this very much as well. However, there clearly are other key factors in our decisions of going for one job over another, around the status a job gives you for example, the type of work, seeing the opportunities to evolve over time, where a job might lead us to. Tell me what you think but to me it feels like it goes beyond finding a job that is meaningful and provides fun.

MR: I think we, at least some, are willing to put a little bit aside, and give less importance to salary for example for other things. If you tell me 'you will have a fixed schedule, you are going to do XYZ, and no longer what you have been enjoying doing, but you are going to earn a third more', there is a strong possibility that I am going to say 'Thank you but no thank you'. It is possible than 20 years ago, in the same situation, I would have said 'yes, who cares, I'll make more money'. I really think that we are valuing more our time, our passion, what we learn and what we do, and if you feel you are being challenged. Of course this only applies to one type of workers. Of course, I am not saying that everyone has this chance. I believe this group I belong to, Eidi and you belong to, is the luckiest group, a group with good education, with languages, we have opportunities. 80% of the population is probably not that lucky and have fewer possibilities.

Interviewer: I am working in an environment where I see in practice what you are talking about, feeling that element of choice, but I am also working with people doing similar jobs, but from different generations, and some are driven by very different things. Do you see this in your environment, and if yes, does that create any tensions between generations?

MR: Of course it happens. The older people I interact with, the generation of my Dad or Grandma, really value stability over everything else. Stability is one of the core elements, as you need to bring money to support your family, you are responsible for that. They don't fully understand other ways of working. My Dad for example, I probably told him about a hundred times what I did for a living, and yet, he does not really understand it. He wonders how come on a Thursday morning I am working from home. It just does not make any sense to him. Or how can I be in Lima on Tuesday and south of Chile on Wednesday and taking Thursday off. To him, this is just impossible. So yes, between generations of course it is different, the values are different. It has changed for more of a focus on entrepreneurship and flexibility. Or game. I am really convinced that nowadays, you can get the most of the organisation in general if you make them play! If people are having fun, they will be getting involved and achieve better results, financially. Does that create tensions? Yes, probably. Where I work, there is an environment where the average age is about forty and everyone thinks along the same lines but I can imagine that in more diverse environment you can find some of those tensions.

Interviewer: I'd just like to come back on what you were saying on the idea of 'playing'. Organisations as I tend to see them today are 'serious' places so to say. Having worked in an Anglo-Saxon environment, I found it actually quite relaxed, you are typically better off starting a presentation or a meeting with a good word or a joke. Now working in a French environment, I found it much more serious, and not necessarily in a good way. Playing, having fun, exploring does not particularly relate to the behaviours I see fostered and valued. I agree with you that we should see much more of that but it sounds paradoxical in today's organisations. Play and fun is not part of most organisations' DNA and how they function, although quite a few see the added value this could bring.

MR: Well, that is the reason why I started studying cultural biology. I am doing a Master's degree, led by a famous biologist, Umberto Maturana, and he brings most of his ideas from biology. This is not based on psychology or sociology, but on biology. At the heart of what we are and where we come from, we do play. We, as humans, are made to play, and organisations will get the most of us, focusing on that particular aspect, to enjoy, collaborating with one another, to bring the best of us where we feel comfortable, precious, when we feel someone cares. When that happens, we as human beings bring the best of ourselves. Competition, strict rules, places where you are constrained; they 'cut your legs'. That way of being goes against our human nature. I see what you are saying and see as well that most organisations are behaving in a very serious way where playing sounds like something you would just never do but I am now reflecting on how we could do things the other way around. The whole human nature is based on the idea that us, as human beings, care about each other. We like to be around people, we like to play and those environments bring the best of us.

Interviewer: Have you seen specific studies showing this? Maybe that in playing, one is faster at resolving problems, maybe learning better too?

MR: Well, what I am reading at the moment is very biological, so it not necessarily about that, but what I am going to write for my thesis, is how do you create those spaces for collaboration, how do you create environments allowing collaborative behaviours to emerge. Collaboration is not something you can force and if you try to force it, it does not happen. That said, you do have to create 'the space in between' so collaboration can emerge. I am convinced that if collaboration truly happens, this is better for just everyone, for the well-being of people, as well as for the results of the company. You can get people more innovative, more loyal, which is particularly challenging today as people are moving around. They last two years in a job and they want to move around. How do you get people to be loyal, to be creative, to be innovative, to work together and to have fun? I think it has to do with creating the space to play, to collaborate. Organisations act as big shadows in a way that when they are really strict, with rules, it allows you to behave only in certain ways, organisations constrain some parts of what individuals could give, they shadow you, you cannot shine, all the good stuff cannot come out. Let's say you are a very good surfer in your own time. There are many great things you learn being on a wave, such as balance for example, that you could apply to organisations. If you like doing magic tricks in your free time, focusing people's attention on particular elements, this is also something that you can apply to organisations. And people can then better connect to their organisation: 'that thing I love about surfing, I can do as well in my job'. And then, they can shine.

Interviewer: Funny that you should say organisations do not foster that today. I'm working with a few companies really trying to get that space for people to bring their own selves, personalities, and specificities at work, and provide a platform for this. I see a real steer from a few leading organisations to allow more of that.

MR: Yes, I think you are right, it is happening. There are a few of them, not many. Places where you can bring your passion to the office in a way. If you think about Google for example, where there is such a creative environment, or Pixar, those companies do think hard about how to create those environments, and things happen. The difficulty I find is to convince the people in charge that if you do this and invest in it, it is going to be better for the organisation. Typically, we'll hear those are 'softy' ideas, 'you just want people to have fun and to be happy'. That is not the point at all. If you allow people to shine, you'll create a space for people to have a better life but also, it is going to bring out better results. That's very much connected! That's very much the way I want to drive the work I am currently doing with the team, the OD team we are building. I was working in a more old fashion way before. Now I think I should approach that differently, look at it up-side-down. I am not sure how yet.

Interviewer: For the last 10 minutes that we have, I'd like to touch on another topic Eidi explores in her narrative: the changes currently taking place in your part of the world, or the stability, and instability of the political context in Latin America. How do you see the world of work evolving in Latin America, and in particular in Chile?

MR: If you look at the Chilean history of the last 20 years, you'll see it is probably one of the most stable countries in Latin America. We are a little bit different from the rest. What that means is that you don't see here as much uncertainty as you would in Argentina, in Brazil, in Colombia or in Venezuela for example. But the political context does indeed influence work a lot. Right now, there is a very flexible understanding of careers, at least for the mobile workers I belong to. The chances that I have to go away and find a job are probably a thousand times higher than it was 30 years ago! The chances for people to move away are down to individual choice. The choice is in their hands. It is really easy, especially for good workers, or the big thinkers, doctors, PhDs or whatever. As soon as they feel that the country is not safe enough, they'll likely move away. And that's clearly more of an option today than yesterday. A while ago, it would have been impossible for me to come to work in France or in the UK, now it is not difficult at all, and especially because of the crisis that just happened a few years ago in Europe.

Chile is full of Spanish people now. They came because they had no jobs in Spain. So what you mentioned around the stability and instability in Latin America, is it the same thing that happened in Europe a few years ago, especially in Spain.

Interviewer: So do you think, in terms of the trend in Chile versus Mexico for example, that you see the emergence of more flexible workers?

MR: Yes, of course. This very much applies to mobile workers, because many others do not have this chance at all. Chile, for investors, is quite appealing. Mexico is a dangerous place, I would think twice if I were offered a job there. They have this 'on' and 'off' way of living. I would never go to Venezuela for example, Argentina would feel very unstable. In Bolivia they won't even take us. Lima is growing, but it remains a smaller population, at least compared to Santiago. I feel very lucky that I am part of that specific group of the population. Although people are saying that Chile is growing - it is growing every year by 3 to 5% - the country remains very unequal. The differences between the rich and the poor are devastating. Conditions in Chile differ a lot. As a family, if you earn 2500 USD, you belong to the top 10%, the richest people. Within that 10%, there are some people insanely rich! But 90% of the population is not.

Interviewer: Manuel, we are coming to the end of our time together. Do you have any closing thoughts?

MR: What I am really into, what is really taking my thoughts nowadays is this idea of collaboration, innovation and well-being. I am really absorbed by the idea that if you allow or build the space for people to join, to collaborate, to be themselves, bring the passion into their work, it is going to be better, not only for them but for organisations as well. It is going to bring long term results. Identify reasons why professionals start behaving as they do now is not easy to find. There are many different reasons. Organisations have to transform in order to allow for people to shine and allow them to be who they are, think what they want. Things are changing. Organisations should change too.

Interviewer: Thank you for your time Manuel.

PART 3:

In Search of a Proportionate Passion

In Search of a Proportionate Passion

Toru Jhaveri

"Rest in reason; move in passion"

Khalil Gibran(1923)[34]

A few words on Toru

Toru Jhaveri is a psychologist who took what she thought would be a detour from academia to work as a qualitative market researcher with the Nielsen Company. It has been eight years since, and she is now a brand strategist at one of India's leading advertising agencies. She is passionate about creativity, culture, writing and dot-connecting and enjoys the unique combination of methods and madness that typifies agency life. She lives and works in Mumbai, India.

Toru believes that work-life balance is a construct that is lived, embodied and negotiated by people over time and that there is much more to it than 'time-management' and 'multi-tasking.' In

[34] Gibran, K. (1923). The Prophet. New York: Knopf.

which case, doing what you love and loving what you do can prove to be very mixed blessings indeed. Which accounts for the peculiar angst of the privileged Millennial who is lucky enough to pursue work that she wants to do, but isn't equipped with the tools to decode the full implications of such wanting.

Learning passion

Passion: Celebrated by culture

Online quotable quotes libraries throw up hundreds, if not thousands of quotes about the importance of doing what you love, loving what you do, and the sense of fulfilment that comes from having spent a day engaging in work that inspires and enthuses you. Attributions for these quotes range from ancient Buddhist texts to artists, writers, scientists, actors, to geek-gurus who change the world, including the one-of-a-kind Steve Jobs, who famously proclaimed that *'The only way to do great work is to love what you do'*. A passion for one's work is a recurring theme in the biographies of great men and women, in graduation addresses and more prosaically, in HR leaflets and motivational workshops.

I'm not sure which religious or spiritual tradition can lay claim to either inventing, or reasonably approximating the idea of *'Work is worship',* but I can attest that the role of work in life is a cornerstone of some tenets of ancient Vedic and early Hindu spirituality. This spiritual tradition sometimes conflates the ideas of work and duty, and suggests that karma - action - work, when engaged in as duty and done selflessly, without expectation of reward, is a route to understanding and seeing higher truths, and possibly (although this might be a stretch) leads enlightenment.

Looking at people at the absolute zenith of their fields - the giants in technology, sociology, psychology, design, and advertising on whose shoulders I stood in the course of my work practically every day - seeing how driven and animated they were by their ideas and obvious sense of purpose, it was difficult not to aspire to a similar level of enthusiasm and inspiration about one's work.

Passion: Learnt at home

My culture celebrated work. And so did my family. Apart from the odd professional, occasional medical student or bank employee, my mid-sized (by Indian standards) family consisted almost entirely of entrepreneurs and businesspeople, many of whom had built their businesses from scratch. They had enjoyed some success, been occasionally burnt by failures, and identified to a large extent - if not completely - with what they did. Those who were members of longer running family businesses took pride in continuing personal traditions and building on small legacies.

Profit was important, of course. It would not be an exaggeration to say that it was the *point* of undertaking a venture or running a business. To that end we would always celebrate Diwali, the Hindu New Year, going through elaborate rites and ceremonies to worship and welcome home Lakshmi, the Goddess of Prosperity. But work was also much more than a means to an end. It was personal, it endowed a person with purpose, and it was valued for its own sake.

Passion: Art and ideal

What I absorbed at home was reinforced by my interests in art and music. Visiting local galleries week after week, I learnt about the Indian Modernists, artists who were very much *avant garde* and provocative within the country in their time, and who challenged the boundaries of what could constitute art and representation. Like great artists everywhere, they experienced struggle and strife, relying on aid from friends and family to tide over financially. They were driven by passion and an eagerness to experiment. Years later, prosperity and recognition caught up with many - but not all - of them.

Further afield were the European frame-breakers - Van Gogh, Picasso, Munch and many others who personified the ideal of the genius consumed by an overriding passion. Reading about them in textbooks and museum workshops, it was easy to construct a romantic, if somewhat fanciful biography of them as men engaged in the noble pursuit of beauty as truth for its own sake. As a young student, these accounts - part fact, part myth - seemed to promise a salvation-grade purity of purpose that more prosaic kinds of work and less inflamed emotions just couldn't.

In parallel, my lessons in Hindustani classical music were punctuated by stories about great singers and instrumentalists who had devoted a lifetime to their craft and practised it relentlessly. One of my teachers memorably said that I should dream in music. Well aware of the limits of my abilities, I decided it was probably alright if I didn't.

Growing up amidst these myriad influences - the stories about music, art and artists, the inculcation of the values of hard work and dedication, the pop cultural and quasi-spiritual value attached to immersing oneself in a profession that was almost a 'calling,' it seemed to go without saying that whatever I did - and I was free to choose what that would be - I would have to do it for the right reasons and with commitment. As assumptions go, it was an inspiring one, a license to explore, to learn and to find work that would excite me.

Enacting passion

Passion: Making unfashionable choices

Buoyed by family and teachers, I took these early lessons on work, commitment and fulfilment and ran with them, studying the deeply unfashionable subjects of Psychology and Literature, following up with a Master's degree in Organisational Psychology as opposed to the more vocationally oriented and better known courses in Human Resources and Industrial Relations.

As in my studies, so too in my career, which has taken an atypical turn. My decisions about 'what to do' were guided less by what would be lucrative, and more by what I thought would be interesting. I spent three years working as a qualitative market researcher and now work as a strategy planner in one of India's largest advertising agencies. When I started working, neither were these professions 'trendy', nor did they promise financial rewards beyond measure. So what drew me to the work and kept me going?

It was the fact that I saw my career as an exercise in learning how to join the dots, in testing myself intellectually, in acquiring new perspectives and new skills. My choices had less to do with pay cheques and designations than with learning opportunities. Implicit, perhaps, was the desire to take the road (relatively) less travelled, to echo, in some small way, the artistic heroes of my youth by taking the risks my parents had been too sensible to take.

As a qualitative researcher, I spent hours talking to people, analysing data to arrive at patterns and themes. I learnt how to question, how to listen, how to manage project logistics, teams and deadlines. As a strategy planner, I stitch consumer insights, category developments and cultural trends together into brand strategy for my clients and intellectual capital for my agency.

The picture I look at has gotten larger and the impact of the recommendations I make has correspondingly become broader. It is easy to become cynical about working in advertising. The popular fashion is to critique capitalism and advertising is of course one of the great engines of the market, so it comes in for a significant amount of scepticism. Working in advertising is a choice many feel defensive about, but I enjoy participating in the creation of tangible and intangible value.

Passion: Being unfashionably earnest

My professional decisions and learning were also accompanied by a 'bright-eyed and bushy-tailed' approach more suited to interns than to seasoned, hard-nosed professionals. If there was a new experience to be had, I wanted to be a part of it. If there was a new consumer segment to be analysed, a proposal to be written, a new business pitch to be run, a methodology or analytical framework to be explored, I wanted to be involved. I would come early, stay late, juggle three, if not four, if not five balls in the air, burn my cylinders and take work home - mentally, if not physically. Deconstructing and solving a complicated problem or knot seemed like the most logical thing to do with any spare time or energy that I had.

Enacting my earnestness was made easier by the fact that in India, the boundaries between personal time and work hours were blurred to the point of being non-existent. There was, and continues to be an assumption that a professional/employee will always be available. In the experience of many young professionals, there was little respect for the concept of holidays without interruptions and un-intruded 'downtime'. Technology was expected to help accommodate the growing demands of a job rather than making them more manageable. And 'facetime' - the scourge of organisational psychologists everywhere - was the index of choice in assessing commitment and value in a competitive job market.

Passion: An enabling infrastructure

What I wanted from work was to be engaged and challenged, for my mind to be stretched and used in different ways. I had a great fear of becoming a unidimensional professional, one who could only deconstruct and solve a problem in two or three ways.

Which is why, what I sought out from my manager(s) was input, to be pushed along a learning curve. Happy to assume responsibilities, I wanted them to relate to my own goals and objectives in some way and to be made part of the working equation as an individual. I also believed in the power of good working relationships - I was old enough to understand that not all colleagues could be friends, but it was important to me to have mutual respect and regard for what each colleague brought to the table - whether it was experience, a work ethic, the ability to diffuse tension, the ability to bring out the best in others.

Like most people, I thrived under managers who gave me freedom to make decisions, the autonomy to set my own goals and schedules and who threw me the occasional curveball. That my company had ambitions for me that matched my ambitions for myself was reassuring. Getting sent for regular training was reassuring. Hearing positive feedback, was, I must admit, more than a little reassuring.

But what I wasn't paying enough attention to were the signals mentors were sending me about slowing down and cutting myself some slack - the occasional tangential comment about 'perfect being the enemy of good,' which soon evolved into more direct comments on 'taking it easier' and then, just, 'taking it easy.' It was a situation so clichéd that I didn't even recognize it, in spite of my studies in organisational psychology - the enthusiastic young professional was taking her work and work-goals more seriously than she needed to.

Rationalizing passion

Passion: Put into perspective

It was one thing to go full-tilt at a job in which I was running projects with a significant degree of control. My managers and supervisors were quick to step in whenever there was a problem, or to give me input either when I sought it out, or towards the closure of assignments and deliverables. But the assumption was that I could - and would - operate more or less on my own, or within a small team of people who knew me, and whom I knew from close to three years of working together and understanding one another's requirements and quirks.

As a qualitative researcher, my projects proceeded linearly, with one step leading to another, clearly adding up to a presentation which was supposed to leave the clients with a deep and insightful understanding of their consumers, either broadly or in relation to a specific business and perceptual query. We collaborated with quantitative researchers but only infrequently, operating more or less as an independent unit with our own purpose and role.

But advertising was a whole different ball game. I was thrown into cross-functional teams, often numbering several people, each of whom had a point of view not just on what they were supposed to do, but on how I should function. My output no longer stood on its own, as a whole - it built on inputs from others, and was crystallized into briefs or positioning opportunities that were intended to get copywriters and art directors inspired and enthused. My presentations had to be strategically sound, rigorous and interesting, but they could no longer exist independent of creative ideas and creative work.

And then there were the meetings - many, many meetings and conversations which seemed redundant to me but essential to several others in the room. Advertising had its deadlines, and they were demanding, but that didn't stop people from hovering around and over a point until they were completely satisfied that they were, in fact, completely satisfied. Work proceeded in circles. Two steps forward one day, three steps back the third, with a final mad scramble towards the finish line on day zero.

As a qualitative researcher, I needed to be efficient, productive and effective. It wasn't that these requirements were irrelevant to my work in advertising. But I would definitely need to redefine them.

These changes were unsettling but also interesting. I enjoyed the conversations, the collaborations, the thought that something I had heard or read or said could spark someone else's curiosity and creativity. Interacting with a wider and more diverse set of people was stimulating and sometimes, just plain fun. Working late into the night on a new business pitch, it felt oddly comforting to know that whatever I was doing, I wasn't in it alone.

But teamwork could also be frustrating. It meant that I had to take into account a whole set of variables that I could no longer control - a colleague's perspective or cognitive style, a peer's habit of scheduling meetings without checking whether the timelines worked, others' evident disinterest in what was happening or being discussed. Some colleagues were reliable, others less so. Some cared about producing the best possible piece of communication;

others had different and equally valid priorities - such as maintaining client relationships or managing their stretched teams' workloads. If I had an opinion, so did others. If I had five other things to do, someone else had seven.

The baseline was constantly shifting; the moving parts of our machine were always in motion. Somewhere along the line, after trying to 'organize' and 'orchestrate' small things in small ways that seemed meaningful and significant to me, running up against difference or just plain indifference, being alternately thrilled by someone's support and completely put off by another's lack of engagement, I realized that I was expecting the impossible - that everyone would bring to the table what I needed, with what I considered to be the appropriate level of interest and intensity.

Ultimately, after a period of some frustration and annoyance, it dawned on me that the passion that drove me in specific and particular ways would not always animate my colleagues. And that my expression of interest in work could not always be about me - it would have to make space for others - their motivations, their varying levels of interest and ability, their willingness to lend support in their own way. I wasn't interested in control as much as cooperation and it became apparent that I would have to leave room to negotiate its terms. These negotiations could go either way: bringing delight, or disappointment.

Passion: Better spread thin

My lesson in difference and flexibility was accompanied by the less gradual but no less important realization that I liked my work best when it wasn't the only thing I was doing. I had sporadically taken courses alongside full-time work, shoe-horning class and study time into my schedule over weekends and late nights. It could seem overwhelming at times, but having a completely new idea, construct or piece of information playing on my mind was much more appealing than grappling with work-related preoccupations, seven days a week.

I have recently taken the resolution to make this occasional practice into a life policy. It doesn't even have to be a course of study - it could a concerted effort to explore a new art form (this year, theatre with very limited success) or the determination to reinvigorate latent interests (reading - I picked up fiction after a five month drought and haven't looked back). And as much as I hate having to resort to cliché, the truth is that having multiple interests and many sources of intellectual ferment has made me a better professional. An unexpected bonus, if you will.

And finally: A proportionate passion

A proportionate passion: Work as one part of life

We all negotiate the demands of work in distinct ways, some with greater adaptability than others. Some people see work as a 'job' that is to be done for x number of hours per day in return for financial rewards that allow them to live an inspired and full life on the weekends. Others are more driven by the work itself and don't necessarily perceive a dichotomy between work and life. A lot of people subscribe to the idea of work-life balance, which reminds me of mathematical formulae, almost as if inadequacies in one sphere will be compensated for or cancelled out by a surplus in the other.

For my part, I believe that 'work-life' as a term sets up an opposition between work and (non-work) living that is artificial. After all, work is very much a part of life. So if you treat work as if it's separate from living, then that means more than half the hours in the week have been spent having no life at all! Which seems absurd. Work gives me routine, it gives me challenges, it is a fodder for conversations, for friendships and minor enmities, it is a source of very particular pleasures and pains.

So work is something, but not everything. Not opposed to life and living, but not a substitute for life and living either, not the sole engine of my motivation and fulfilment, and certainly not the place where my best instincts go to hibernate. It allows me to express certain aspects of myself but it is also not the arena where my personhood and sense of worth are negotiated.

Was it Starbucks that said that they wanted to be the customers' third place, wedged somewhere between work and home? Work is a place for me, certainly an important one. But I would be very disappointed if it were the only one.

A proportionate passion: Conceding control

Treating work as one part of life has gone hand-in-hand with my acceptance of the limits of my efforts and powers. I have some influence and credibility, which I try to put to what I believe is good use, but I recognize that I am not controlling anyone, or anything, beyond my own output. Conceding the illusion of control is incredibly empowering - it liberates me from the attempt to individually manage and deliver collective outcomes, but it also puts me in a position to choose where and how I direct my energies. It teaches me to work with what is, rather than with what should be.

This has made me more present, aware, practical and effective - when I no longer expend energy worrying about things that could be or should be, I have the resources at my disposal to deal with things as they are and to involve others in getting things done in ways that we collectively believe are productive. I try to focus on my teams instead of issues at the client's end. I try to attend to small tangible changes that can be made instead of big ideals that are never going to be implemented. I try to think in terms of solutions rather than problems. Conceding control can mean losing some battles. And then realising that they weren't battles at all.

A proportionate passion: Selective detachment

Selective detachment is about many things - knowing when to switch off is the first among them. Advertising is an industry with long hours, working weekends, an overlap of the personal and professional. The boundaries are very blurred. Moreover, the job market is so competitive that facetime becomes a crucial way in which to show commitment.

No one is waiting to hand balance over to you on a platter, it's something you must define and pursue for yourself. Which, for me, means not thinking about work when I don't need to. This also means that when I am working, that is what I am entirely focused on, choosing to detach from other things in order to get assignments done.

Equally important is knowing when to move on from working relationships, either with individuals or with organisations. When it comes to individuals, employees must know whose feedback to value, and to what extent. This is particularly true of creative industries like advertising, where egos can be fragile and perceptions of the quality of someone's work can be largely subjective. A lot of people in advertising will admit that while we work for our clients, we seek respect from our peers - they are the ones who truly understand the craft and thinking that separates good ads from great ads. A client might reject a piece of work, but that doesn't mean it lacked worth. At the same time, having output approved doesn't signify that it couldn't have been many, many times better.

When it comes to organisations, relationships are built on a foundation of trust and mutual regard. Particularly at the start of one's career, it is great to know that someone with more experience and wisdom is looking out for you or willing to give you the right advice. Trustworthiness earns loyalty and the willingness to go the extra mile. It's impossible to put a price on trust, but it can make people work harder and with more joy. On the other hand, inadequate communication, opaque language, a concern with hierarchy and dominance and assertions of power or strength, a use of official channels to 'score points' are all signals that something's not quite right and that it might be difficult to be happy at work. In which case, what options does one have?

Many people are unhappy at work. They want to be able to demonstrate ability and work with people they respect and with organisations who respect them. And yet, when they encounter difficulties in achieving a balance at work, the response is cynicism and stasis rather than a positive effort at change.

I fully acknowledge that there are times when it's smarter to stay in a bad job than look for a better one. But when the option to look out without sustaining significant financial or career damage is available, selective detachment gives a person the momentum to take it. Or to use that time to learn something new or maybe just experience the world differently. The reality of the working world may have changed to some extent, but the coping mechanisms people are using - disengagement, staying safe, 'managing' till an alternative becomes apparent - belong to a past generation.

Selective detachment can help a person perceive situations objectively and stay one step ahead - of themselves and their habits, more than anyone or anything else.

A proportionate passion: An on-going process

Being proportionately passionate sounds terribly Zen. It is anything but. For me, it is a constant refrain, a lesson always in the learning, mistakes always in the un-making. Being proportionately passionate is the way I try to extract the maximum joy and pleasure from what I do without limiting myself to being defined and consumed by it. It is a recovering perfectionist's formula to counter perfectionism's many ills. Being proportionately passionate makes me a better employee, and I think, a pleasanter person. It's a struggle, but one I believe that's worth having.

A proportionate passion: The bigger picture

The question of passion at work is also one we need to debate in larger forums and on bigger platforms. As I mentioned earlier, Millennials who can choose what they want to do, who can pursue their passions and seek meaning in their work are truly, genuinely privileged. But there is also a price to be paid for this privilege - that of identifying too greatly with a passion or pursuit; of not knowing how to accommodate life's many demands while one is gainfully employed; of 'expressing' oneself in a work situation at the cost of others' expectations and needs; of becoming suspicious of any work-related demands that seem predictable and routine; of enacting a sense of entitlement at work. These can be easily dismissed as first-world or one-percent problems, but that would be to miss the point.

The rhetoric of passion at work is powerful, infectious and most importantly, aspirational. It could very well shape the form our organisations take. It might be where young people outside the hierarchies of privilege locate their ambitions. It is an ideal that has currency, and therefore, calls for debate and investigation.

Discussing the narrative with Daphna Salomon

"Work is like love, there is no substitute for chemistry"

A few words on Daphna

Daphna is a creative content & design freelance-consultant. She helps businesses and individuals articulate, frame, deliver and engage with messaging in a strategic and powerful way. She produces and collaborates on content including scripts and articles, as well as the design of space that facilitates learning, decision making and pivotal conversation. She is passionate about innovation, cultural exchange, creativity and the psychology of design.

Daphna is an explorer of the working world and of the world at large. Her free spirit takes her to many unexpected places.

Interview transcripts

Interviewer: Can you tell me a little about what you do now - and what brought you to this point?

Daphna Salomon (DS): Before joining my current role, I worked at an HR consulting firm for approximately two and a half years. The role was closely related to what I had studied - Organisational and Social Psychology at the LSE. It was a steep learning curve at the time, and I had gained significant knowledge and experience, however two years in I felt I had reached a plateau, and felt saturated. I decided to take some time to recalibrate, personally and professionally, and really think about what I wanted to do next.

Now I work as a consultant at a creative agency that specialises in all things internal communications; designing events, communications and brand strategy, creative content, engagement. In terms of what I envisioned from a job, it checks almost every box. Everything is great on paper. But, I learned that work can be a little like love, there is no substitute for chemistry. On paper, this role was perfect- on paper, it still is. But in reality, real life happens between the lines, and for the past few months I have been thinking: 'Is this the route that I should have taken?'.

The chemistry is missing. I mean all the ingredients in the pot are good- the vision, the salary, the good manager. But how it all comes together, the experience that binds it all, falls short. Call it culture, call it unrealistic expectations. I call it chemistry. It's not enough to put the right ingredients into the pot, the magic is in the final experience.

There's a lot of talk about what cultivates discretionary effort and what makes people want to go that extra mile. We know about the importance of leadership, having a good manager and having alignment with the nature of your work. All of that is really, really important but at the end of the day there's also something which can't be singled out in such a way.

Interviewer: I see. Tell me, have you worked prior to these positions that you've told me about, or is it that you went to the LSE right after your undergraduate studies?

DS: I had worked in the time between my undergraduate and postgraduate, as well as before university. From communications work at a large pharmaceuticals company, to an Operations Manager role at Tate Modern and Tate Britain, to research at a think tank that bridges the private and public sector. I've had quite a few positions before coming to this role. On the surface, they've been different to one another, but I can see a connecting thread between them. I'm still looking for the right path.

Interviewer: That's interesting. Can you tell me more about what made you choose these roles at the time? Was it something that excited you? Was that the willingness to try something new? Maybe just the people you met, did you think that they would teach you something? What drew you to them?

DS: I was drawn to each of the roles for different reasons. The first role that I took after my undergraduate degree involved museums and heritage sites. My degree was in Communications, Media and Culture and I got involved in the communication of culture front and education of the public, which I loved. I was exploring the practice of the things I had learnt in theory. I enjoyed being part of an education process. The roles after that had a similar vein, in terms of pushing an education agenda. The think tank sought to shed light on what talent looks like in Britain, and how it shapes the economy and workforce dynamics. I was getting involved in a process where people were learning from the things that I was doing. That's what felt good.

Interviewer: Would you say that that's what drives you when it comes to work? What is it that really makes you want to wake up in the morning and do whatever it is that you do?

DS: I wish I had a stellar answer for you, full of conviction and passion. But the truth is I think that it changes with age. When I was younger, like many people, I had some very big ambitions - not ambitions in terms of changing the world but I really wanted to have a big impact in some form. I thought if I don't make a significant impact, then there's no point in my being. I almost felt like I had a duty to ensure I did something to make the world or society better. Grand ideas. I think the older I got, the more it dawned on me significant doesn't necessarily mean on a massive scale. I basically realised that the term 'impact' comes in all shapes and sizes and forms, and having a serious positive influence on a the people around you can be just as rewarding, important and dutiful. So my will and desire to impact is the same, but my understanding or my perception of what that impact is and means, has changed. I am no longer looking for the big scale footprint. I just want to feel like I am adding value and helping people around me have more meaning in their lives. That drives my own meaning. So my perception of what drives me, has fundamentally stayed the same, but the way that it's being applied that has shifted, with age and with experience.

Interviewer: I think it's interesting that you say that. Because I do quite a bit of consumer work in the work that I do, and when you talk to young people, particularly when they're in their teens or early twenties, their ideas for what they want for themselves are pretty grandiose. And it takes a while for the sense that small change is meaningful, it takes a while for that to percolate, and for that to be a legitimate driver for work.

But, what do you think being passionate about work is? It's such a loaded term. Different people have a different sense of what it means - for some, motivation, drive and passion are all more or less the same thing. For you, what do you think the term connotes?

DS: I think that passion is the fuel, but care is the vehicle. I'm driven by things that I care about. This brings me back to where I am at the moment, and perhaps contributes to the reasons that I'm not sure I'll stay in the long run. Ultimately I thought educating, stimulating and stretching myself could be enough, but at the end of the day, I am finding that I don't genuinely care enough about the things I am producing here, designing these events and programmes. It's easy to dress it up, make it sound really cool, sexy and exciting, I can use all the buzzwords that people need to hear to bulk it up. But deep down, I know, that I don't care enough about it, or believe in its supposed value, for it to really move me. Once I care about something, I'm all in.

Interviewer: So, in all the work that you have done, is there a particular project or a particular instance when you felt that this fuel was really burning? You had the perfect moment, or perfect vehicle, or the perfect incentive to feel passionate and bring passion into what you bring? Do you feel like you've had that particular high point in your career which you feel you'd want to benchmark your other experiences against?

DS: I think I've had a few, and actually they've been in very different contexts. For example, when I was consulting for the HR consultancy, I went to deliver a client presentation. I was sitting in a room with the CEO, and his entourage, five or six VPs if you will. We were discussing the transition that they were going through as an organisation, and it was apparent that it was failing quite miserably. During our conversation, it emerged that their underlying organisational culture was basically crumbling from the inside. It was clear that we needed to change many things and a lot of that had to do with the new CEO. The new CEO felt he was letting his people down and didn't know what to do about it, and we carried out some very heartfelt and challenging conversations. I was in the room with six leaders having a very human-level conversation, that would see impact on the business. It was very empowering. Through facilitating a genuine personal exchange and connection, navigating through people and politics, we would shape business outcomes. What surprised me, looking back as I hadn't given it thought at the time, was that a large factor of what transpired was due to the fact that I allowed myself to just be me, as I am, without the business consulting hat on. I was able to make a very strong personal connection with someone and I made an impact on him personally as an individual. He just happened to be the CEO, who impacts an entire business.

There's another example where a team member confided in me about something very personal and I was trying to help out and trying to find a way that this person could stay within the organisation and still attend to some personal needs. My role in this situation was equally as impactful, and served the person and the organisation. I don't know if that answers your question, but basically when I genuinely care about the process and feel my input could produce genuine impact then my passion pushes through.

Interviewer: It is interesting that you approach it that way. When I got into this conversation I would have assumed that people will talk about passion and they will talk about the big things. Like the conversation you had with the CEO where the intervention is very high profile, and the impact is very tangible. But I see a couple of interesting threads coming together in this conversation, and I will pursue those a little. You said something earlier about being Jewish Israeli and that passion comes naturally to you. Can you tell me a little bit more about that? Is it that you are expressive, or get committed to causes and values?

DS: It is important to make a distinction between Jewish and Israeli. There is a difference. Talking about 'Jewish people' is a very broad brush-stroke term to use. Within the Jewish community there are many different ways of interpreting and observing your Jewish-ness. But something that does connect throughout is the dedication to education, and the notion of taking care of your community. Historically Jews have invested in skills which are mobile and can be transferred from one place to another. Adaptation, critical thinking and awareness of the surrounding environment. So that's from the Jewish point of view, which is less relevant to the point- but bringing the Israeli point of view to the fore is a whole other conversation. Israel is a small state, in size and population. it's a competitive society and a breeding ground for entrepreneurship and innovation. That is most likely symptomatic of its geo-political, social, economic, cultural melting-pot, securityincentivised psyche. People are passionate and critical. For good and bad, but it is not called the Start-Up Nation for nothing.

All this lends itself to how Israelis are in general, it's the way they operate in everyday life, and it also translates to how they are at work. The reality that exists in Israel basically creates a climate, where people have to both physically and mentally survive, and thrive. They are critical thinkers, are fast and efficient at assessing contingency plans, and alternative scenarios. Plan B,C and D. They are usually very opinionated, which can come across as arrogant. But overall, authentic. The drive is to improve, self and the surroundings. These are important traits to bring to businesses. And even though it can be experienced as abrasive, ultimately it can bring a huge amount of value if there is someone listening.

I too have been viewed as critical, even argumentative. Mainly expressive, as you mentioned. However, in an Israeli's mind this is usually considered a healthy debate, an essential process for improvement. Passion, underlines it all.

Interviewer: That's interesting what you said about entrepreneurship and I guess about an environment cultivating a certain kind of resilience and a certain kind of energy. So I was wondering, because very often when people talk about a work ethic or an approach to work or an understanding of work, it's equal parts personality, part of what they inherit from culture - even though they don't know it - and part also a legacy that they inherit from family and parents. I come from a family that's very entrepreneurial, I am just about the second person in my family to have a job, and everyone's sort of waiting for me to take this job and use it as a stepping stone and an opportunity to run my own business, for instance. So I was just wondering whether there is an understanding of work or a relationship to work that you may have sort of osmotically acquired from parents, from siblings, uncles, aunts, influential people in your childhood?

DS: There isn't a particular work mode that was cultivated or encouraged in my family. We are four siblings, and two of us work as employees, and the other two have their own business entities which they own and govern. My parents believe in finding the fine line between financial security, and self-fulfilment and heart. It's a hard line to negotiate, as we know, one usually overpowers the other.. unless you are very lucky, and you really do what you love. Which is what we all strive for.

Interviewer: OK. The topic of my paper is around finding 'proportionate passion', and something that I've written about is that it's wonderful to be passionate, you're encouraged to be passionate. In my family as well the assumption was always that because there was a certain level of financial stability, my sister and I would find work that really inspired us and enthused us because we had the ability to make that choice. And that was great and it was a wonderful freedom to have, but at the same time when you're passionate about something or driven, it's very hard to know when to stop or when to switch off, and to achieve this mythical thing called work-life balance, which I don't even know if it really exists, but that's definitely something I wanted to talk about. What's your perspective on it - as an organizational psychologist, as someone who's done so many different things. Is there such a thing as being able to power down when you're passionate about work? And how would you do it?

DS: Powering down passion, interesting. Work life balance is a huge topic for debate. The influencing factors change with age, experience, role as bread-winner in the family, and gender in my opinion. There was a time in my life where I knew I had to go full-power because I was building the foundations of my professional career and skills I felt would serve me in the long run. These were formative years , and I was working very, very long hours, at the clear expense of other things. I decided there would be time to nurture those other things later. But later, brought a host of new challenges. Priorities change, and other aspects of life gain more or less relevance and gravity as you mature. I missed important occasions in those earlier years to dedicate time to work. Nobody from the company I worked for remembers those missed occasions, but I do. Proportionate passion is a great term, and I think the key is sustainability. Busting the engine is expensive. High cost in terms of time, well-being, health and longevity of my working life.

I am also not disciplined in keeping clear boundaries between work and home. I bring my work, home. And that is unhealthy and upsets the balance of proportionality. I think this is an on-going struggle, that varies in complexity and difficulty for our generation. It has to do with so many factors; social politics, organisational policies, gender, glass ceiling, tech, as well as emphasis on wellbeing in the work place, for the workplace. A proportionate passion is certainly something to aspire to.

Interviewer: I'm glad that I had this conversation with you, because one of the things that I felt for myself was that this negotiation of balance is a process, you keep thinking of it as this place that you reach, but it isn't. It's something that you're always looking for, and you're always defining it and re-defining it and asserting your need for it and you know, you put your foot on the accelerator and then you pick it off again and I'm at a slightly different life-stage, but already I feel that it's easy to get consumed by work, in this particular stage, in 20s and 30s, so it's important to step out of that. And I don't know how many of us are able to do it successfully, even though we claim that that's what we want. So those were my questions. We are now coming at the end of our time together. Thank you Daphna.

PART 4:

Questioning my Current Paradigm

Questioning my Current Paradigm

Jen Lu

"Choose a job you love, and you will never have to work a day in your life."
Confucius (551-479 BC)

A few words on Jen

Jen is a 30 year-old woman living in England. She grew up in the Netherlands, but has lived in various places in Europe since age eighteen. At age twenty-four, she moved back to the Netherlands and took a position as a PhD researcher in applied psychology.

After completing her PhD, she moved to England for her current job as a researcher at a London-based university. As a psychologist, her work focuses on the role of behaviour in addressing a variety of societal problems.

Why work?

Work is such an integral part of my life it is difficult to say what exactly I think of it. I do not question why I go to work. Sometimes I am excited and other times I am demotivated, but most of the time I simply work and get a quiet sense of satisfaction out of it. Although I believe many things besides work are important in my life, for the time being, I cannot imagine living without the purpose, structure and routine it provides. A sense of purpose is important to keep me going, but without structure and routine my life would probably turn into a daily struggle. Despite its repetitive, routine-like qualities, similar to life in general, I also see working life as a journey. I embarked on this journey seventeen years ago and hopefully it will continue for at least another three if not four decades.

Gen Y growing up

During my formative years in the booming 1990s, the discourse of self-actualisation through work was in its heyday. I remember the career adviser at my secondary school – who was also my personal mentor – telling us about his career switch and the yearning for personal fulfilment in his working life. He posed us a simple question: 'what is important to you?' Although some cocky teenage boys shouted 'money' in reply, most concurred that intrinsic motivation was important. Ultimately, 'what do you like doing?' seemed to be a more relevant question than 'what will get you a job?' and 'what will generate a generous cash flow?' After all, why would we, children of the bright, shining future, ever have to worry about job security and making ends meet?

Having said that, I should probably mention that I took my first part-time job as a thirteen-year old and continued having part-time jobs for the remainder of my school years and summer jobs throughout my student years. Although I didn't need to work to meet my living costs, I have been aware of the connection between work and money for much longer than my number of years in full-time employment suggest. In other words, I have never been naïve about the practical value of work and have executed many menial tasks in the name of work during my formative years. I also did not choose to pursue a career in subject matters that are notoriously difficult to find a job in. This is not to say that my choice reflects a trade-off between interest and job security, but there are plenty of degrees I ruled out from the start that might have been equally 'interesting'. However, I did change my mind about the direction of my career halfway through my degree. While I initially did not consider research as a career option, my love for the subject eventually convinced me to go down the academic route.

The question my career adviser posed might have been simple, but not easy. My short answer to the question has remained unchanged over the years. I do not consider pay and job security to be the most important features of my work. My long answer, however, has changed. In addition to what interests me and what I find meaningful, I have realised the value of a nurturing working environment, work-life balance and the importance of recognition and reward. It is difficult to know precisely how much of this is due to the mere process of growing up or the changed economic circumstances, but I am certain the latter has played a substantial role.

Work during a world crisis

I believe the economic crisis has limited the opportunities I have had during my working life so far. When I was looking for opportunities to do a PhD in the Netherlands in 2007, research budgets of universities had already tightened and competition appeared to be fiercer than ever. I decided I had to compromise on pay and place of residence if I wanted a swift move. Soon after I started my PhD, however, I realised the way in which the university was realising my pay cut and overall reduction in costs through a scholarship was highly controversial, and in fact, a form of tax evasion. PhD 'students' are usually considered employees in the Netherlands which comes with all the related benefits (e.g. pension schemes and other employment-related benefits) and duties (e.g. tax payment).

I ended up unleashing a course of events which eventually led to heads rolling. On a personal level, I was appalled by the way some organisational members responded to my legitimate concerns. As a psychologist, I was for the first time consciously observing and analysing power dynamics at work. The Foucauldian idea of power as relational and the inherent possibility of resistance all of a sudden turned from an abstract concept in a textbook into something I experienced in real life. During this episode, I realised that 'the organisation' as an entity as such did not exist. I talked to many different people within the university and their response varied enormously. The manager with whom I first raised the issue with more or less explicitly blackmailed me and suggested I should keep quiet. However, I soon found people in formal or informal advisory roles who were a lot more supportive and helped me throughout this whole period of uncertainty. The top management of the university eventually engaged with my problem which led to a generally reasonable solution, namely converting the scholarship to an employment contract. The lesson I learnt from this episode was that negotiation is a key organisational process. It cannot be assumed that rules and policies are set in stone. Representations of such rules and policies vary between organisational members and can be manipulated to exercise power for the better or the worse.

University politics apart, the economic crisis also affected my perception of job security. Although I have not been unemployed for a single day, friends and colleagues around me have struggled to find a job and stay in their chosen professions. The suffering that can result from this is heart-breaking and I am aware that I have been lucky to escape the more severe consequences of the economic crisis. However, it is because of the very fact that I felt that job security could not be taken for granted, that I was very proactive in seeking employment. After my PhD, I relocated once again in order to stay in academia. Also, when I was unhappy with the organisational culture at my workplace, I was reluctant to give up my job and seek my fortune elsewhere. I am now happier with my job than I was at the start. I made peace with the dominant organisational culture, at least for the time being. In order to work with those whose views of work and cooperation I do not necessarily share, I have found it tremendously helpful to see their strengths, not only their weaknesses. Although it is true that I am mainly staying put because I feel working on my track record is more important than the organisational environment I am working in, I am still enjoying the work and appreciate the positive aspects of the organisational culture. There is certainly an element of risk aversion, but I would like to think the tougher economic climate has also brought out personal qualities such as grit, discipline and humility.

I also believe the economic crisis – and the banking crisis in particular – has shed critical light on the function of organisations in society and ultimately the value of our jobs. How do our organisations affect society? What role am I playing in this? Despite the fact that universities in the UK have been affected by a pay freeze and all kinds of cuts, I do not see colleagues moving to the private sector en masse. In fact, I see people moving into academia in search for meaningful employment. The strength of people's intrinsic motivations should not be underestimated. Income really does affect one's standard of living in an expensive city affected by ever increasing property prices. I am not suggesting that work in the private sector is not meaningful. My point is that the meaning we attach to our work can prevent us from taking up better paid or more secure jobs elsewhere.

Leadership

As obvious as it may sound, I have come to recognise that leadership plays a crucial role in how I feel about almost every aspect of my work. It makes the difference between what looks like a dream job on paper and a fantastic job in reality. As much as job content matters, without the right support and guidance from managers, everything becomes a chore. Leadership can be a facilitator or an obstacle to employee productivity, performance and satisfaction in many ways. If a manager has valuable expertise and experience which they can and are willing to share, it can be a huge boon to employee development. Perhaps even more important, however, is a manager's ability to motivate employees and shape the right working conditions under which they can flourish.

In my field, it is rare to find employees with no or little interest in their work. Nevertheless, motivation can wax and wane. There have been moments when I felt ashamed of my lack of motivation to do my work. When I dug deeper into why I was feeling demotivated, it was usually an inability to do my job effectively or unfair treatment. Adequate resources can have an impact on motivation because they help to boost productivity, which in turn fosters a sense of accomplishment. Resources can come in many forms. Money, knowledge, professional networks are the more obvious examples of resources, but organisational policies and informal rules, such as the ways employees are expected to work can all be stepping stones or stumbling blocks. In my view, it is the manager's role to ensure the availability and fair distribution of resources to the best of their ability. I am explicitly mentioning fairness because it seems to be the source of much discontent. While perceptions of fairness will invariably differ, aiming for fairness should be the goal. I have often found that the lack of transparency fostered a sense of unfairness. Why can one employee work from home but not another? Why do some get to travel to nice conference destinations more often than others? How did the manager arrive at these decisions? Fairness is also about recognition. Appropriate recognition in formal or informal ways can give a boost to motivation.

None of this is rocket science, but it is definitely easier said than done. So far in my career I have experienced two leaders whom I perceive to be opposites of each other. I shall name them Mary and John. Both are experts in their respective fields, but Mary's expertise was not as relevant to my specific job as John's was. As a result, I often had to rely on my own good judgement while working under Mary and approach other experts proactively. In contrast, I have received a lot of input from John and have learned very much from his feedback and have also been able to make use of existing collaborative partnerships that have given access to data that I otherwise would not have had. Although I have learned more from John directly and have benefited from established partnerships, Mary has made more use of her network to help me, even when there were no existing partnerships. Mary was also more willing to provide material resources to facilitate my work.

Perhaps most important of all though, is that Mary's and John's leadership style are diametrically opposed to each other. Mary is happy for her employees to work from home any time they want and generally limits feedback on a piece of work to a minimum. John has many rules concerning office hours and other aspects of life in the office and gives extensive feedback on work. When I started working under John, it struck me by thunder when he said he would normally expect people to be present in the office, but did not question where some of his long-time employees were. This gave me two signals: one, I am the one to adapt to him and not the other way around; and two, I am not to be trusted as a new employee.

Another specific issue I have had with his leadership is a lack of recognition. For example, John makes unilateral decisions about authorship of our publications, so I am never certain if and to what extent my efforts will be suitably recognised by authorship. It is done fairly most of the time, but there have been a number of occasions when my contribution was not appropriately recognised in my eyes. There was no option for appeal which has left me distrusting and more detached from my work. I think the more general, underlying issue is his understanding of the relationship between managers and employees, and junior and more senior employees. To me, it is cooperation, no matter how much individuals differ in 'rank'. This is not to say that I do not respect the opinion and experience of my seniors, but I should not have the impression that decisions are made based on their whims and idiosyncratic preferences.

You can tell from the way I have described these two people's leadership styles that I prefer Mary's by far. As a matter of fact, I do believe that her leadership has certainly had a far more positive influence on my motivation and (possibly to a lesser extent) my performance. When I feel supported and am given appropriate recognition and responsibility, I work harder and – at least that is how it feels to me – it seems to sharpen my mind. However, everything has its flipside. The lack of structure provided by Mary's leadership style meant that unless you had the discipline and motivation yourself, you were unlikely to get that extra push you might need. Also, John's involvement in my work resulted in a steep learning curve for me because I could witness the thought processes of an expert who has a few decades more experience under his belt than that I do.

Leadership at large

Universities tend to be loose conglomerations of faculties, departments and research groups. It is usually the last unit, the research group that academics tend to identify themselves most with. So I am not entirely sure what I actually want from top management. My first response would be: not much. However, it is not true if I consider that 'my' manager, or the manager of 'my' manager, is more directly influenced by the organisation's top management. In a way, similar expectations apply to both top and middle management. Of course, a key responsibility of top management is to attract adequate resources and maintain a good reputation for the organisation as a whole. It is also the responsibility of top management to facilitate and guide middle management's role. At least in the context of universities, it seems there is too little harmonisation of human resource policies which leaves too much room for the personal preferences and judgements of individual 'managers'. Although there is something to be said for flexibility and decisions case-by-case, top management should balance excesses. Good academics are not necessarily good managers. In organisations where managers have usually acquired their position through expertise in their subject matter rather than management skills, it is important to have appropriate checks and balances in place.

Cultural diversity

As someone who works and lives in a foreign country myself, one particularly exciting development in the workplace is the increased occurrence of transnational employment. At my previous workplace in my home country, I had foreign colleagues from various nationalities, so I have had experience on both sides. I am glad to have had these opportunities and truly believe contact with people from different backgrounds enriches our lives. Nevertheless, it also seems to be a source of tension because of the way cultural values and practices are entrenched in our psyche. It is a learning process, which is not a bad thing per se. However, in many organisations, there is often one (usually local) culture that dominates the workplace. It is therefore the minorities who adapt, without their presence having any significant impact on the majority. As a result, any possible benefits of diversity within the workforce are likely to be limited as well. I do not have hard data to support my beliefs, it is just my experience, which may or may not be generalisable to other multicultural working environments. I have felt the complacency when I was part of the majority group and the pressure to adapt when I was the odd one out.

To illustrate my point, consider these two contrasting experiences. When I was still working in the Netherlands, I once had a conversation with some of my foreign colleagues who believed it would upset relations with management by having a frank discussion about an issue that was perceived to be a bit thorny. I told them that they would never get what they wanted or needed if they were not upfront about their needs and demands. Twelve months down the line, one of these colleagues admitted he had learned the hard way that he needed to be direct. Generally speaking, it pays off to be assertive in a Dutch working environment. Once I moved to England, I noticed that colleagues rarely said anything that went against the opinion of the head of the research group. At first, I believed it to be a rather silly norm, but soon I experienced the negative repercussions of doing otherwise. Now, I have learned to nod my head, smile and say amen.

Balance

It is precisely because work plays such a large role in our lives that we want many, sometimes contradictory things from it. We want to grow within our professional roles, but we also want to be comfortable and do not always appreciate the pressure that comes from challenges. Do I stick to things that I have done before and can do efficiently? Or do I take on new tasks that require more effort and entail more risk of failure? Similarly, there is a seemingly inherent tension between work and life. Of course, it should be about 'balance'.

The beauty of academic research is the freedom it often provides, although – as I discussed earlier – the extent of this can vary greatly between departments. Output can definitely not be measured by the hour and there are no precise criteria for how much work needs to be done and the quality of that work. The flip side of this is that it is always possible to do more and to do it better. For instance, how many publications do I need? How much time and effort should I put into each one of my publications? Is it worth checking my analyses one more time? In short, when do I say, enough is enough? Of course, it is not just up to me to decide, but the lack of clear rules means that there is a tendency to do just that little extra which also entails another evening or weekend spent in the office.

More generally, when there is a great opportunity up for grabs, the question is whether the extra work can be reconciled with a mere 40-hour working week. Can you be ambitious and have a nine-to-five job? In the short term, my personal experience is that imbalances are a necessary evil. It is impossible to turn off the computer at five o'clock when deadlines are looming or inspiration hits. In the long term, however, the opposite seems to be true. Without time off, mental and physical fatigue eventually set in and productivity declines. I do not consider time off as a luxury. Although working conditions are far worse for some people in the past and in the present, my experience is that it is simply impossible to do my job as an academic researcher well if I do not take some rest from time to time. Neither do I think my conviction is specific to Gen Ys. I have had conversations with people from the baby boomer and war generations who have had experience doing work that relies heavily on cognitive functions and they concur.

Gender equality

One specific 'balance' issue is gender equality in the workplace. As a child, I told my nanny and my mother that when I'd grow up, I would buy a big house and have five children for them to take care of. I clearly did not see the necessity of raising my own children. Now I'm a grown-up, I wonder if it is possible to combine work with childcare. My native country has one of the highest proportions of part-time working women and also at my current workplace in London there are part-time working female colleagues who have children. Still, it does not address the issue of whether it is possible to have a 'proper' career and raise children at the same time. Of course, it all depends on one's definition of a 'career' and there is nothing wrong with having priorities other than work. The real question is if you have the drive to 'excel' or reach 'the top', can you realise these ambitions and simultaneously work on Project Family? That is, if you are a woman. To me, gender equality would, among others, entail that the choice to have children would equally affect men and women, but it clearly does not at this moment in time. While it is certainly possible to negotiate childcare responsibilities within each individual family, I think it would be naïve to believe that most of this is down to individual choice. Without changes in family policies, politics and society at large, there will be difficult trade-offs one has to make. Childcare is not only about gender equality though. It also raises another fundamental question about whether our attitude towards work should be challenged. Why should work be a reason for someone not to have children? What does this say about our values and views of human life? People will invariably disagree on the precise answer and it should not be about imposing our own values on the rest of the world. However, asking these questions may help expose unchallenged assumptions underlying common practices.

Beyond personal experience: observations of others' at work and in life

I am not a work psychologist, but I have interviewed many employees about related topics for my research and met people from all walks of life who have shared their views about work with me. From my casual observation, the differences between people are large and small at the same time. On the one hand, we are all human beings who need their basic needs to be met. The needs I am referring to include but are not limited to food, shelter, a degree of security, and social recognition. From the investment banker to the aspiring artist and the NGO employee, everyone values a pay check and colleagues and managers they get on with. The extent to which we value each of these seems to vary though. When I talk to people working for businesses, some – I hasten to say not all – openly declare that financial reward is the most important feature of their job. Although I personally would like to think it is not, the disagreement is only a matter of degree. I also get annoyed by the pay freeze of academic salaries, requests for personal contributions to our yearly Christmas party and washing-up liquid in the office kitchen and the large pay gap between academia and other equivalent jobs. I am not ashamed to say so because I believe we should get rid of the idea that some jobs are of a 'charitable' nature which allows for a different set of rules to apply. Employee recognition and compensation should be universal and not limited to profit-generating corporations. People whose role is to serve the public good should not have to rely solely on altruistic and other 'intrinsic' motivations to keep them going. Conversely, we should also not have to rely on bonuses to keep corporate employees on the job. This is of course a gross overgeneralisation of reality. My point is that, at this moment in time, there seems to be an imbalance between the various universal human needs that are normally met through jobs from different sectors.

The discourse of corporate social responsibility (CSR) is therefore a welcome one. When I was interviewing employees from a range of different organisations about CSR-related issues, I noticed there were different views within each organisation and things were never black or white, but typically grey. It is all too easy to become cynical and believe CSR is merely window-dressing. While we would probably be too optimistic to expect motivations other than profit and personal gain to dominate corporate strategy one day, I believe CSR could be a valuable tool in achieving a balance and containing excesses.

The crystal ball

I am a believer of life as one big experiment. At this moment in time, I am still aiming to develop my full potential in my current role as a researcher. Although I want to contribute to the greater good, personal growth is at least equally important if not more important to me. When I look back at the end of my career, there would be nothing worse than seeing that I have stagnated most or all of my working life. As a researcher in a junior role, I feel I do not always have the opportunities to develop a diverse range of skills. Next year, I will contemplate which direction I want to take my career in. Knowing that I am likely to stay in the workforce for at least another three to four decades, I am keen to get a taste for life outside academia. Academic research tends to involve long-term projects and the output needs to be 'sold' to an expert target audience. To get a different perspective, it would be insightful to work in a different sector. Perhaps I will love it and never look back, or I might go back to academia, having learned from my experiences elsewhere. Another direction I might pursue is teaching. The few teaching opportunities I have had so far have been challenging, but also very engaging and stimulating. These ideas for the next career step have in common the desire to be more directly involved in delivering a service or product with more tangible beneficiaries. It is likely that a move into one of those directions will also result in better job security or pay. If so, these would be very welcome side effects.

Work is a popular topic in the public domain and it is my hope that all discussions and critical reflection will eventually lead to improvements and allow people to have more fulfilling lives and working lives in particular. At present, we know in theory that work-life balance, personal development and growth, recognition and reward, diversity and corporate social responsibility are important. However, we are often merely paying lip service to these principles. We will only act accordingly, if we truly believe that adhering to these principles will lead to the best outcomes in the long-term. Confucius might have been right that choosing a job you love means you will never have to work a day in your life. But what makes you love your job?

Discussing the narrative with Ása Ludviksdottir

"Work is not going to catch you when you fall."

A few words on Ása

Ása has a Bachelor of Science degree in Mechanical and Industrial Engineering and a Master in Organisational and Social Psychology. She currently holds the position of a Director of R&D Analysis, in the R&D department of Össur, a global company in non-invasive orthopaedics, where she has worked for over 7 years. Main responsibilities include the rolling forecast budgeting of the R&D department, preparing R&D monthly reporting to the executive committee and taking a seat in the R&D management team.

Previous roles include, manager of Clinical Research within the same company, were she was responsible for testing new medical devices with end users to verify product functionality and safety. Before that she was a Risk Management Specialist within Kaupthing bank for 4 years, focusing on minimizing the bank's operational losses.

Interview transcripts

Interviewer: Can you tell me a little bit about your work - what you're doing now, and what you did before, maybe even before you came to the LSE?

Ása Ludviksdottir (AL): I work for a global company headquartered in Iceland, and it is a company that develops and manufactures medical devices, mainly artificial legs for the lower limbs, and various braces, neck collars, that kind of thing. In my current role I am an R&D office manager, which involves focusing on R&D operational responsibilities like the R&D financial forecasting and developing our Key Performance Indicators, regarding how to monitor and report our progress. I sit in the R&D Management team and in my work I collaborate closely with the team. Right now there is also a project I am working on, developing a more formal innovation strategy for the R&D department which I really enjoy. So, work is diverse and it is fun, and I work with numbers and work with people and am developing different tools. I think it's great.

Interviewer: And what were you doing before this? It was more of a pure research role, a research protocol role, if I'm right.

AL: Yes, I was a clinical research manager, and what that involved was working closely with different people in the R&D team, overseeing the testing of new products on end users.

Interviewer: I wanted to talk a little bit about the meaning of work in your life, and what exactly does work mean to you, and what role does it play?

AL: Work is quite important for me. It is something that gives purpose, it gives a routine, but also, it gives me plenty of worth so to say, and I am not sure that this is a good thing. For example, after working hard to complete some important project or a milestone, I feel good about myself, I feel like everything is working out well in my life. I am not sure that's right - but I think that's what drives workaholics at work. You feel good about your accomplishments at work, and that's what keeps your focus there. You work more and you feel even better, and you don't have time to deal with the other things in your life. And it is tempting to go there.

Interviewer: Right. And do you worry about it, actively?

AL: Well, I am aware of it. I don't think it's running my life. But I am aware of it, and I try to not let it take over, basically.

Interviewer: That's interesting, because I'm doing two interviews, and the other person that I spoke to was very driven about work. And I find it interesting what you say, that it's supposed to be really good to derive a sense of accomplishment from work, but that there's something dangerous about it as well. So when have you noticed it and how have you tried to not let it take over - was there a specific project where you felt you were going too far in the direction of work defining you?

AL: It kind of happened over time, but I care about work-life balance. I have many friends and I have a really nice life, outside of work, I have hobbies and things that I truly enjoy. At one point work is just taking too much space. I guess it is a very delicate balance, and it comes in circle too, it starts with one interesting project at work, and more effort, it means more projects at work, and even more interesting projects, and the more fun it gets, it means less time that I have left for my personal life. So it is a constant trade-off, a constant compromise.

Basically, you have to stay on your toes and give work enough to get all the exciting projects, but not at the cost of all the rest. And if I fall into the habit of working too much, when I finally have free time then I don't know what to do with it, I've fallen out of practice to have free time, so to speak. What I'm trying to do now is to organize myself better at work and that's helping. I am trying to do more work in the same amount of time, be smarter about my time, and I feel there is lots more room for improvement when it comes to time management efficiency, and I am trying to tackle it.

Interviewer: So it's almost like you can manage your time better, if you think about what you want to do outside of work.

AL: Yes, and I feel work-life balance is just the core, because that's what it is all about, really, to have an acceptable work-life balance, because obviously work is not going to give you complete fulfilment in your life, and if you start working too much you also start losing yourself and that's not what you want.

Interviewer: And what is it that you look for from work? What motivates you? Because you were saying that you were looking for balance on one hand but work also gives you some sense of purpose.

AL: I think it's really evolving; it's like, playing with clay. It is almost like being at university or something. In the past, it was about completing projects based on deadlines, doing my duty – its work after all and has to be done quickly and efficiently – that kind of attitude, and not really thinking about developing myself as an employee on the way and more importantly, not allowing myself to make the effort to turn it into something truly enjoyable.

Today, it is about learning and enjoying and finding the aspects of my work that I find truly interesting, and it is also just as much about having a good relationship with co-workers and to reach out and give them a hand when needed. This is where I am now and I think that change is good for me and for the company. I am taking a different perspective now.

Interviewer: When did this start changing? When did you make that shift from wanting to complete a project to actually wanting to relate better to people, or to do more different things?

AL: I think it just dawned on me, as I worked, and it's what I'd learnt, as a child. I was an 'A' type of student, I received recognition and praise for having good grades, and this kind of reinforced my effort to work hard and keep on receiving good grades. There was no focus on really learning something that evoked my interest or that I enjoyed, instead I put pressure on myself to accomplish something that other people or the school system wanted me to accomplish, not something that gave me fulfilment. And I kept this up because I got awards, I got appreciation, which I liked. And then it kind of dawned on me that this is not sustainable in the long run, to have my worth and drive linked to duty and praise, it has to be something else, it has to be enjoyment, it has to be something that has my interest. That's the only way.

But it took a long time, because for a long time I had taken work really seriously, and very literally. I think this shift of not taking work that seriously to try instead to enjoy it, has made me more effective, because the more you keep things in perspective, the more you don't take things personally, it's not your life, and the outcome is a better place.

Interviewer: Was it a particular incident, or someone who influenced you, or was it just an internal shift?

AL: I think it was personal growth, an internal shift, maybe increased self-esteem. I was seeking to grow both in my personal life and in my job, and it was a learning curve. I just realized on the way, but I did not have one moment of clarity or something, no.

Interviewer: It's an important shift. And it's very clear to me when you speak about this that it's not so much about extrinsic motivations. Has it really ever been about financial rewards for you, or has it always been about accomplishment and now, learning and growth?

AL: It's not about financial income except that obviously you have to make a living. It's rather about internal accomplishment and having a sense that what you are doing is important. And it's not just about increased bottom-line in your company's outcome, but that sense that the end result of your work is something that really matters. But I guess that applies to all of us, if we are fortunate enough to be offered that kind of job, everyone would prefer that, I think.

I also feel like, from my job, my work gives me status, but that's also not something that I want to dwell on, because it is not real. What I mean by this is that where you work is not who you are or how good of a person you are. This status I may get may happen just because my company is well known, people keep it in high regards, and it is one of the most popular companies in Iceland. So some people give me status when they know where I work, but I don't want that and try not to pay any attention to it.

Interviewer: So you can't control how people react to that information but you don't want to give it too much importance.

AL: Exactly.

Interviewer: Do you believe that your parents have influenced the way you see your work in any way? Do you think it may come from something in your family or in your culture?

AL: I think it comes from the society, as well as from the culture. Work is really the core of our lives and is really important part of the culture. And you're not as valuable if you're not working, which is obviously not a great attitude. We have a 'working-hard' culture. You start working early in Iceland, you start working maybe when you're 14 and 15, during your 3-4 months long summer vacations. And then you get a job alongside high school and university. And you start taking up more and more work, you work and study during winter and then you also work through the summer. But society looks at you, at how you work. Society then, yes, but I don't know if it comes from my parents at all. I don't know if they really encouraged that. They were of course happy that I was doing well at school, they thought it was great. That kind of reinforced me in the ethic of working hard, and maybe they forgot to tell me to look for what my heart wanted and that interest and enjoyment is fine.

Interviewer: So that's something you had to discover for yourself, to a large extent.

AL: Yes, exactly.

Interviewer: That's really interesting, Ása. I think you're one of the very few people that I talk to who has that kind of awareness. I mean it's very easy to get seduced by this narrative of hard work, right? And you seem to have a lot of clarity about why that may not be the healthiest response in the world, and that's quite unusual. Just to sum up what we just discussed, it seems that when you were younger, or working in previous roles, you were more likely to want to prove yourself, accomplish things, gain approval from a supervisor. But over time, you seemed to have realized that you didn't want to judge yourself using work as a standard. You stopped seeing work as a defining part of who you were. Now, coming back to the question of what it is you seek from your work, how has this changed with time?

AL: Well, in essence I have come to realise that work is only work and you better just enjoy it, and it is just one piece of your life. Although work can give you immense satisfaction and a great sense of achievement, it's only work and that's important to remember, the context of things. Work will not catch you when you fall, and the interests of the organisation are probably not the same as yours. So if you may need to quit your job, you are not left in ruins with no sense of purpose, because you didn’t build your identity and sense of worth based on your work.

Interviewer: That's an interesting way of putting it - that work will not catch you if you fall. Another thing I wanted to talk about again - when did this change start happening? Is it just a function of work experience, or growing older, or seeing people around you? When did you realize that work should not be so important?

AL: I changed my job around a year and a half ago and then I started thinking about things, and I guess that the new job is a more high-level job, it gave me more space, and I realized that it's not all about the little tasks; it's about the whole task.

Interviewer: The bigger picture?

AL: Yes, and I also realized in my new job I had certain responsibilities and I fulfilled them, and if something is needed to be done, I do it. But sometimes, there is a space, I do have some time. And when that happens, I feel now that I can take advantage of the space, so instead of rushing doing the next, most urgent task on the list, I do something I really enjoy.

Interviewer: I understand, and I guess that is because you have a more senior role and the freedom to use your time as you see best, is that correct?

AL: Exactly.

Interviewer: One of the questions I wanted to discuss was how influential is organisational culture, when it comes to work - what are your views on that?

AL: To me, it is really important, the culture. It is almost like first you have to like the person, the company and want to be a part of it. If you don't relate then I really don't see the point. So I mean, that's what it is all about - the culture, it is so important, and it is what makes everything happen.

Interviewer: The culture has to be of a kind of place where you want to belong.

AL: Yes.

Interviewer: And what about organisational culture and work-life balance? What are your opinions on that?

AL: It is connected quite a lot. If it is the kind of culture which values long working hours, and your colleagues are keeping long working hours, then you feel pressured to do the same. So if the emphasis is on how many hours you spend at work instead of the actual delivery of the work, and the output, people may spend more time in the office just to fill up the hours, you know. But culture affects work-life balance.

Interviewer: We just discussed how organisational culture links to how employees feel about work. What about leadership, according to you?

AL: I guess it is very linked to the culture. You have to believe and trust the people of the organisation and believe that they are doing what is right, and you have to be able to identify with your leaders, their goals and values. That is always the case from my experience.

Interviewer: So what about the relationship between leadership and culture - are they one and the same, within an organisation?

AL: I think it's really closely linked. When you have a new leader, or specially a new CEO, it has an impact on the organisational culture. I had a new executive in the unit in which I am working in recently, which changed the culture visibly. I think underlying though, there is something more, there are layers. I think the top layers are more readily influenced by the leaders, the underlying values of the company are more difficult to change, they are more stable and long-lasting.

Interviewer: So you believe that those values are more likely to influence the leader, than the other way around.

AL: Yes, right.

Interviewer: Given the amount of work-experience you have - how successful have you been, according to you, at negotiating work-life balance?

AL: There was a time, there was a period in my life when everything was about work. And it really impoverished my life. And now, this is not the case anymore, and I can say that I am happier as a result, and again, the things that have changed are quite simple. I try not to work too much day to day, I would rather work 8-9 hours a day, and I try to balance the number of projects that I take on. I try to organize things beforehand and set a goal as to what I want to accomplish this week, even every day, so I try to plan. It only takes an hour or so to plan the week. I really feel that because I organize my goals, I am more effective. And I try never to work on weekends if possible. Maybe once every month I can work half a Sunday, but not more than that. However, maybe I use 30 minutes on Sunday to organize the week ahead, but that's all. And then I try also not to check e-mails outside of work. I mean of course sometimes it is needed but not more than one night a week or something. Then while I'm at work, I try to maintain my energy and don't take things personally and maybe not push myself completely to the limit. Take care of me while at work, and remember that it's only work.

Interviewer: Earlier, you said something about how, when you're at work, you try not taking it too personally. Can you talk a little bit more about that?

AL: What was really an eye-opener for me as well. Of course, not everything works out and goes on straight lines. Before, I would be upset, my day would be ruined, almost. Everything becomes so personal. It's better if you remember that it's work, you kind of step out of the immediate context, it expands your view and I think that it improves things. I became a much better worker as a result, because it wasn't as personal.

Interviewer: It's interesting that you say that! When you read books and quotes about work, you're encouraged to make work personal, right? Motivational speaking and all of that is really about loving your job and taking it personally. But what you're saying is really kind of the opposite, is that detaching from it is what makes you a better professional.

AL: I think so, I really love my work, I like that the products we are providing have been helping people improve mobility and quality of life, I really like that. But it's not noble, I'm not at that level, it is a capitalist company and they are trying to increase their return on investment so I know that. So I won't give it all of my heart, only a piece.

Interviewer: So the next question goes in a slightly different direction. It's about resolving conflict, learning how to make compromises and trade-offs. And I think part of what you're saying about work-life balance does involve learning how to make trade-offs, what compromises you are willing to make. Can you tell me about the trade-offs you are willing to make when it comes to work? Let me put it this way with an example - in India, for example, the perception is that the longer hours you work, the faster you will progress in your career, and a lot of young people are willing to make that compromise between balance and a faster promotional cycle. So I'm wondering whether, for you, does work-life balance require some compromise, or is it possible to have it all?

AL: It's like an equation, I mean, work pushes you constantly and wants more and more of your time, but it's not giving back in the same proportion. So you have to find the right balance, when it gives you this fulfilment, and advances your career, but not at the expense of all the rest. But you are the only one that can control it, so you have to push back, not let it push you too hard. And I guess this also maybe relates to not taking work too personally, and also - you have to know yourself, what are your values, never let the work compromise your values. Not become so lost in the culture of the organisation, because you are who you are, above all. Your role as a worker should never completely override your personality.

Interviewer: Right! That's also an important aspect - not just the amount of work you have to do, but the way you're expected to behave, which is also an important part of work-life balance. And that's a part that I don't think we talk enough about, but you're right. I don't think people are talking about balance in terms of being themselves, and staying true and authentic. So Ása, on another topic, you must have people reporting into you - younger people, people at an earlier stage in their career than you. What advice would you want to give someone who is starting out, about this topic? About balance.

AL: I believe you have to find your own balance, not let your company tell you what your balance should be. Listen to your own voice. I think that's really important. Also, you need to do things for the 'right' reasons. Love the job, love what you do, and I was saying earlier, have fun. Do your work well, take pride in doing it well, for the right reasons, but not for someone else or only to get the next promotion. Be true, and don't focus too much on the rat-race.

And maybe one more advice: It took me time to realize that how much you could advance in your career is so much down to relationships, people, and communication. It is not enough to work hard and wait for a promotion, you have to take initiative and let people know that you are suited for that position. I think women, in particular, often don’t feel confident enough to promote themselves. And also regarding relationships, if you need someone to work with you, it’s important to get the person to want to work with you, people don't do things because they have to, most of them do things because they want to. That said, I think it's important to keep in mind that you must stay ‘true’.

Interviewer: Coming to my last question Ása - what are your goals, going forward? Anything you have in mind, something you want to do more of, something you want to do less of. Any thoughts?

AL: Well, I've been in my post for about one and a half year now, and now I am learning the job more and more, and I am creating room for doing other things within the job. I am working on a project where I am doing something really interesting and what I have learnt is that you have to create your own opportunities. It sounds like a real cliché but then I realized this fully. Like now I am working on this project, and it has turned into one of the key projects of R&D department and it is something that I just spotted and this was not something that was handed down to me. It wasn't part of my responsibility but I realized that this is something where we could improve, and I managed to get the management team on board and now it has become a big project and I really like it, and this is just something I created entirely myself.

And that's just how it works, no one is going to hand you the perfect opportunity for you. It's never perfect, it's never going to fit perfectly, I read it somewhere - Lean In - where the author talks about that. You kind of have to adapt to the context, and you can also create opportunities yourself. That's what I am doing - now I am creating space in my job, and now I am more organized, I am learning more, I am just getting better control at doing the things I need to do, so I have more space. To summarize this answer into one, this space I am creating, I am going to focus on creating my own opportunities, on taking initiative, not waiting for someone else to hand it to me, that won't happen.

Interviewer: Thank you Ása!

PART 5:

Finding The Appropriate Fit – For Now

Finding My Way to the Appropriate Fit – For Now – And Deciding To Engage

Ann-Victoire Pincé

"He who would learn to fly one day must first learn to stand and walk and run and climb and dance; one cannot fly into flying."

Friedrich Nietzsche (1891)[35]

A few words on Ann-Victoire:

As an organisational psychologist, Ann-Victoire studies social interactions in the context of organisations. Her passion is to study organisational life and to better understand what makes organisations successful. She is currently working in that field, for a consulting organisation focusing on the different phases of the employee life cycle, helping companies, governments, NGOs to better attract, develop and retrain their workforce. Her particular focus is on helping her clients implementing employee engagement programs, and initiating change in organisations. Her practice is around helping to anchor the intangible, to make it more tangible and use a language which would touch the leaders of an organisation she is advising.

[35] Nietzsche, F. (1891). Thus Spoke Zarathustra.

Ann-Victoire was born and raised in France until she moved to the UK to study and gain some international work experience. After 6 years abroad, she moved back to France, where she is now based.

On the importance of the right fit

'Sink or swim': This is what I heard it was like to work in my current organisation just as I joined. Inviting, right? At the time, being able to swim sounded like quite a challenge in itself. It is only later that I started wondering, what happens once you manage to swim? In other terms, beyond the initial test of whether someone is fit for a job and has the right capacities to perform, what would make them willing to stay with the organisation and go beyond the basic requirements of the job?

During my studies, and being part of that much discussed Generation Y, I was told that the psychological contract between employer and employees was broken. It was most scholars' understanding that, having seen our parents laid off in the successive world crisis, our generation would never trust organisations again to respect their non-formalised duties and responsibilities towards employees - such as providing long term job security. As a consequence, we as Millennials, would not respect ours either - such as remaining in an organisation for our entire career. I was told that my commitment to organisations would be volatile, that we were a generation of individualists, making decisions to build our own careers, independently from any structures, jumping from one place to the other. Some pieces of research seem to corroborate that belief, or at least, many papers state that Millennials have the highest voluntary turnover rate of all generations. Yet, my story thus far proved my teachers wrong.

When looking at that research stream in a little more detail, I realised that a key limitation to most studies is that they compare statistics from people in different age groups, not necessarily from different generations. If we think about it, it is not particularly surprising that people in their fifties are less active in looking for the right job, and the right cultural fit than people in their twenties, since hopefully, after a few years working, they have found and defined their career path. My generation may indeed show high turnover rates, but don't we lack a longer term perspective on this to draw conclusions and generalise this tendency to the entirety of our working life? My gut feeling tells me that we are a generation of individuals who deeply care about our professional activity since our work now represents much more than just a job, but participates in defining who we are, our identity. Considering this as well as the fact that the boundaries between work and personal life are increasingly porous, we try to get it right, and go on a treasure hunt for the 'right fit'.

Actually, the company I am working for has been running a panel study since 1985, asking employees around the world how they feel about their workplace. When looking at the data for employees aged 18 to 25 between 1985 and 2010, we find that Millennials report higher intention to leave their current organisations than the Generation X at their age, but no more than Baby-boomers. Many factors may come into play here, especially the economic boom that our parents experienced in certain markets in the 1980s. The point I am making here is that we often assume that the newest generation entering the workplace are less attached to their organisations, but we lack of strong data to support that fact, and more importantly, some data appear to suggest otherwise.

I feel we ought to be very careful with generational reads of organisations since it might lead to misleading conclusions and particularly to negative or alarming ones. I understand the growing concern of organisations to witness what comes through as a lack of commitment from younger employees, and the specific challenges that this brings. How frustrating it must be to invest time, energy and finances in training, mentoring and up-skilling employees when you are fully aware that this also renders them more bankable and attractive to your competitors. How difficult it must be to grow a high potential employee to a managerial position, and just as he/she is ready for a leadership role, decides to leave for another company. But is that not already happening with the Gen X workforce? Are your competitors not training, up-skilling and growing their employees too? Are those employees not looking for new challenges in other organisations too? Is a bit of voluntary turnover so bad, especially in the early stages of employees' careers?

To me, it appears that the current workforce is indeed more fluid than ever in the past. I also observe in practice what is typically referred to as the emergence of the independent workforce, or the increasing amount of people working independently (e.g. on project based, short term or contractor's contracts). Those changing patterns unquestionably affect the way we think about work and want to experience it. And so, once you have proven that you can 'swim', that you are capable of delivering, what does make the difference between those staying and those leaving? From my experience, finding the appropriate fit with your employer is crucial. What that actually means, I am unsure I can fully define it, but it includes elements around the organisational culture and feeling you belong here. This process is very much a trial and error one which requires time. What has come to me as a surprise is that not only this process of finding a good fit requires time but it is, in fact, a constant redefinition. You find the right fit, for now, but would that equilibrium still exist tomorrow? Most likely not in the exact same way as yesterday. Being aware of those inner changes, reassessing the situation and adapting to any potential emerging needs would be required in order to maintain that equilibrium. It represents a real challenge. However, when a good match is found and maintained for a while it may lead to great outcomes. When I look around me for people who are lucky enough to have found it, I see motivated, committed and trusting employees, and this is how I feel myself – for now.

It took me some time to find a workplace which I felt was right for me. Beyond my first few jobs which provided sustenance, the first career choice I made was to join an organisation which was social and community orientated. I started with what I thought was the most important for me, working for an organisation which aimed at helping people. I was conducting applied research for local communities and believed in the wider contribution of the organisation. Although the work itself was meaningful, I soon started to feel a general lack of passion amongst the team members as well as within the wider field the company worked in. Looking back, it seems that this stemmed from a serious lack of resources and the fact that our actions had very limited impact on the course of how the communities may evolve, almost as if it was not concrete enough. At that point, it was clear to me that I needed something different, something with more passion, more action and greater impact.

I moved from the one end to the other extreme of the spectrum, working in research still, but this time, applied to the world of advertising. I entered the world's largest communication group, in one of their well established and visible companies. I started working on what I originally thought were exciting projects, for large and well-known brands. The working environment was great and I was surrounded with young, fun and energetic people. The company had means and applied those to develop good products, and supporting delivery. It felt like we were doing good work for our customers. Against all odds however, on a personal level, it felt that something was not quite right. I could not see the real purpose behind my work, nor did I see any positive impact of what we were doing. And as in the previous company, I could not feel a shared passion for what we were doing. It felt like people came to work because they needed to, not because their wanted to. What really bothered me was that the company did not seem to contribute to anything else but pushing people to consume more, and that is not something I could fundamentally relate to.

At that stage in my life, I was still living in France and started questioning more deeply what I really wanted to do, but also realising that with my background in psychology, my options were somehow limited in my country. I felt I needed to challenge and push myself further. I felt I could and wanted to do much more and that would require me to leave. I guess, when looking for the right fit, one may also need to take into account our own realities, limitations and sometimes search for opportunities elsewhere, in places not originally considered. This is when I enrolled at the LSE and moved to London.

I am now what we call in a highly 'engaged employee'. Since I started working for my current employer in 2008, I have felt very much attached to the place and believed in what we are doing; I have been willing to do more than what was expected of me, and very much caring for the company's growth and success. Year after year, I have been trying to understand better what drives my engagement. It appears that this company does something right in managing people, or most likely, I have found – for the time being – the appropriate fit. The outcome of it is that I am very receptive to the management style and the actions that my leaders and managers take, and that my memories tend to focus on the positive aspects of my experience with this company.

So, what are those elements that make me stay and commit to the place? I won't dwell on what we may call 'hygiene factors', those elements that need to be covered before we even start talking about engagement: compensation and benefits, safety or employees' working environments. I would rather share elements of organisational life around leadership and managerial behaviours, growth and career opportunities I was given, flexible working options and what I have observed around corporate social responsibility.

Leadership by purpose

What I learned from my previous working experiences is that to sustain my engagement on the longer term, I need 'leadership by purpose': leaders which set a meaningful vision I can relate to and feel they live that vision. I need to be easily able to respond to questions such as 'what is the purpose of our company? What drives us deep down? Does my CEO really cares?'. Whatever an organisation does, there are different ways to go about it, and I need to see that the leadership cares about the mission and vision we set for ourselves. I need to feel that I am not the only one caring about the impact of our work.

With time, I have also realised that I want leaders to manage the business, as successfully as possible, and to communicate openly on how they are going about it. When problems emerge, I'd rather hear: 'we've got a problem, it's going to be tough, but here is how we're planning to tackle it, and here are the implications'. Ideally, I would also hear: 'here is what you can do to help'. I see a general tendency to be willing to share only good news in organisations. From experience, odds are that this would rather harm the employees' level of trust in their leaders than help reinforcing it. As an employee, and referring to Eric Berne's work (1961)[36], I believe we have gone past parent/child relationships in organisations and now is the time to have adult/adult ones established.

Another key element I expect from my leaders is for them to be visible. I need to know who makes key decisions and beyond their name or status on an organisational chart, I need to know who they are. By who they are, I mean what is likely to be on their agenda, and what they would consider the key pillar of the organisation's vision.

[36] Berne, E. (1961). Transactional Analysis in Psychotherapy. New-York: Groove Press

When it comes to creating an environment where employees feel confident about the future of their organisations and trust their leaders, our CEO found a great and innovative way to communicate with us that I would like to share. On top of the traditional communication channels, our CEO sends us one email a day. This is called the 'Thought of the day'.

The principle of the Thought is quite simple, every morning an email awaits for us in our Inbox, coming directly from him. In this email, he may share recent experiences, a client story, some citations from philosophers, some company news, his personal top 5 goals for the quarter, etc. I've kept some of my favourite ones. One said: 'Yes, I sometimes fail, but at least I'm willing to experiment.' (Bono); another 'We make a living by what we get, but we make a life by what we give.' (Winston Churchill). Even though it is of common knowledge in the company that our CEO is not the one either sending or writing the Thought, over the years, the effect on me was quite simple; I have started to feel connected to my CEO. It gave me an indication of the kind of a person he is. What his philosophy is and where his priorities are. It also opened up to the possibility of replying to that email and having a direct channel of communication with my top leader. In reality, I expect that very few people ever wrote back to him, unless of course they had a previously established relationship. Still, this gives me the feeling that my CEO is not a stranger and that he is not far but just an email away.

That is what we could label 'digital leadership'. Of course, trust and confidence cannot emerge from emails only, yet, it may contribute to it if done well and in conjunction with other positive experiences with the leadership team.

Supportive manager(s) providing recognition and treating employees with respect

Now, we do not see our top leaders on a day to day basis. However, we do our manager(s). I have for a long time been a believer that employees – despite what Gallup states – do not 'join organisation but leave managers' (Buckingham & Coffman, 1999)[37]. However, I must admit that my direct manager(s) count(s) in how I feel about working here.

The way we are organised may be a little untypical. Our organisation is as flat as a 3000 people organisation can be and titles have never really existed here. Although I have a line manager – several in fact – our clients are our true bosses. Considering this, I expect my manager to step up and be supportive when needed while respecting my independence in how I do my work. I actually need my manager to trust I would do my best at work, and behave accordingly. I don't think I would do well with micro managing.

Receiving a fair treatment from my manager is a given, even if I see this is not the case in all organisations. Abusive behaviours are just not tolerated within our working culture. The culture we created focuses much more on recognising people for their contribution and providing greater visibility to particularly talented individuals. I must admit that this is what I have seen at my level but many stories have come to my ears portraying the organisation quite differently. Yet, the sub-culture I was immersed in fostered respect and recognition. I would like to share a couple of practical examples.

---

[37] Buckingham, M., & Coffman, C. (1999). First, Break All the Rules. New York, NY: Simon & Schuster.

Maybe due to our performance orientated and meritocratic culture, recognition is quite outward focused. Since our bosses are, in fact, our clients, the leadership has put in place a recognition system based on the feedback received from our customers. In order to be eligible for this award, a client must send directly to the employee's manager an unsolicited email to detail and thank for a particular achievement. Every quarter, awards are announced globally by an email coming directly from the CEO. This provides great internal visibility and pride for the work accomplished.

When someone has done something noticeable, managers frequently send emails to their own managers, copying the employee, to recognise the efforts and contribution made. I find this recognition vital, yet since I moved back to France, I can feel that in comparison with what I have witnessed in Anglo-Saxon countries, the level of cynicism towards informal recognition has risen around me. It appears much harder to instil a more positive managerial culture. My perspective remains that most people – me included - like to feel that their contribution does not go unnoticed and that when someone does something well, the rest of the group should know what great looks like.

Now, to be impactful, recognition must be meaningful. The right balance between too much versus too little recognition must be found. Recognising every single achievement, regardless of neither the impact it may have on the business, nor the development stage at which an employee is would render recognitions meaningless. This also means that the audience of the recognition must be right. Managers should identify how and by whom their employees like to be recognised, as well as who they want to know about it.

Opportunities for personal growth and development

The company where I work today prides itself in saying that opportunities exist here, you just need to go and find it. At the risk of being over simplistic, this sends the following message: we need go-getters because we don't have the appropriate structure or support needed yet to bring opportunities to you, but if you are a go-getter, you will strive here. Not surprisingly then, we have not always been great at identifying talent and growing people in a structured way. However, over the years, I have witnessed many examples of people building successful careers and growing in an impressive and sometimes surprising way. Some decided to expand their skills, others to take on extra responsibilities. Being the witness of those journeys has been motivating and engaging for me. Looking back at my own journey in this organisation, it is likely that the opportunities I have been offered – or taken – were driven by the contingencies of a fast growing company. For years, we have had double digit growth, which, inevitably brings about interesting prospects.

After a few months in the organisation, I was given increasingly complex projects, dealing with extremely demanding and challenging clients, and coordinating large project teams. Very quickly, I was given the chance to enter boardrooms and engage in conversations with our clients' top leadership. I was basically thrown into the deep end, as we do. Beyond finding myself at the right place at the right time so I could get important growth opportunities, I was very fortunate to be surrounded by amazing colleagues who, whenever needed, stepped in and helped me in feeling better equipped. It is interesting how many organisations seem to heavily rely on their employees' altruistic tendencies and coping strategies to self-organise and ultimately, survive as a team.

Working here actually requires a constant reinvention, since our business, our clients and markets evolve, we do need to adapt to new demands. That too brings about opportunities. For a few years now, the market in France has opened and we felt we needed to expand our presence there. This was very timely since I had started considering going back to France myself. The win-win situation we were in made it all happen very quickly and I don't think I had ever seen this company being so nimble. Within a month it was all sorted, I was working on a French contract, from Paris. Now, working in an established market in a large office with effective processes and a myriad of resources versus working at building a reputation, growing – almost creating really - a market, teaching the industry and building a team is not quite the same job. This has been such an exciting time. We were two people that the company trusted to, almost from scratch, establish a business. At the time, we had no clients, no local team, no tools or material in the local language, no name on the market. It was just us. I would define this experience has very much entrepreneurial, and as such has been enriching and stretching.

Moving back to France I was surprised to see how employees would talk about their organisations and how they expect organisations to behave. The sense of 'rights' is much higher than what I have seen in other countries. Organisations here seem to owe their employees. On the opposite, I was stunned to see how low the sense of duty was. From my perspective, on the balance of work, those notions of 'duty' and 'right' should find equilibrium. I very much feel a sense of duty towards my organisation, just as much I feel that my company should match what I give and giving back. Over the years, I have given time and energy to my employer and so far, I have felt they gave back to me, supporting my growth, my development, giving me opportunities as well as recognition.

On flexible working patterns

By now, I presume it is quite clear: I am quite into my job. I find it interesting and challenging and both are equally important to me. It gives me a sense that what I do is useful, meaningful and that the day to day routine does not actually feel like routine. I find the people I work with on a daily basis competent, fun, open minded and willing to work hard. The level of teamwork is well balanced with more individual time. In summary, both the job in itself and the people with whom I work make me feel, once more, that this is the right fit. On top of this, I am given high levels of flexibility in my working pattern. What I might appreciate the most when it comes to flexibility is probably that I am trusted to do the right things at the right time.

Trusting employees appears as difficult for a company than for employees to really trust their leadership. If I cannot see people working, how can I be sure that they are? Well, maybe one does not need to be sure they are, but rather, trust people to be conscientious enough to do the right thing. If a few years ago, organisations were warned about flexible working, most papers now explore the dangers, for employees, of working from home. It appears that people working from home start their day earlier, feel guilty any time they go up for coffee and end up never truly switching off.

Reality is, in our industry – as for most industries today I presume – we don't really have the choice but to work flexibly, and organisations do have to challenge their current ways of working and open up to alternatives. Why? Simply because our clients require it, and because they are responding to their own market conditions too. Beyond the market needs, the apparition of digital tools enabling flexibility, and people willingness to be more agile in their working pattern, we are limited by our infrastructures. We are expecting the world population to grow to over 9 billion by 2050. How are we going to accommodate for those additional workers considering the current saturation of roads and public transportations? Alternatives are needed. Face time is hugely detrimental, not only for employees' self-esteem, for organisational productivity, but also for the society at large. People should be able to get to work earlier, or later in the day, there is a need for people being able to work from where they live. And this is already happening of course. Many organisations allow those alternative working patterns, but do they *really* do it? What I have seen in practice is that when organisations allow for flexible working options, it rarely comes with true trust in employees, true empowerment, but rather with negative perception of those benefiting from flexible arrangements and on the long run, constitutes a barrier to employees' career progression. Flexibility happens in practice, but the old mind-set remains well anchored. Behaviours are evolving but the attitudes behind those behaviours have not yet been modified. Isn't time to take flexible working to the next level?

From a more personal perspective, I see that in the last few years, we became very much used to adjust elements around us to make them more adapted to our needs, rather than changing who we are or how we like to do things to adapt to the world. We can customise just about anything around us. This very likely impacted the way I see my work, and flexibility has become an important part of differentiating a good working environment to a less attractive one. I just cannot imagine working for a company not providing alternative options. To get the best out of me, I need to feel trusted to make the right choices, even if it does include a couple of adjustments on how I do things. I am being asked to be flexible in my deliverables, and if I am flexible, my employer should be too.

Organisations behaving in an ethical and responsible manner

The importance of working for a company that behaves in an ethical and responsible manner might not be as important for all, and probably was not the key factor in getting me interested in joining the company, but it clearly plays a part in how I feel about working here and in retaining me as an employee.

The reason why I am personally attached to my company's commitment to contributing to the community may come from my background. Although both my parents are business orientated people and successful entrepreneurs, some hippy tendencies remain from their twenties, and had some impact on how they wanted to raise their kids. They enrolled their three children in an alternative school, where we followed the national curricula; however our teachers strongly focused on children's individual needs, allowed for exploring more artistic topics such as theatre, singing, painting, dancing, and so on. Part of that teaching is about opening up to others, helping one another and contributing to the community. It is likely due to that education that after a few years of working for a capitalist organisation, I felt an urge to do more than running a few races here and there to raise funds for charity and to contribute to something greater. At some point I lost touch with the wider perspective on what I was doing on a day to day basis and could no longer see the 'meaning' that I had found for years. I guess I needed to see more tangibly the implications of my work.

Luckily, my company gave me the opportunity to do so by participating in what was called the 'Time to Care' program. The program allows employees to leave their employment to work for NGOs, up to 3 months, while being paid as usual. In order to join the program, I had to convince a committee of the value of my project, explain the reasons why I had selected a specific organisation and not another, and had to explain specifically what I will be doing and how this will then benefit me in my practice. This program is based on trust, 100%. I was not asked to provide a detailed report, or sign a paper which tied me to the organisation for another X months, and that is an element I strongly appreciated about it. I trust my company, and my company trusts me in return.

I then left for 3 months, and worked for a French based not-for-profit organisation aiming at supporting other NGOs working in the field of international solidarity, either in western countries, or in developing areas in providing consulting services. It is a network of professional consultants, working in other consultancies, who intervene on several missions based on their specific competencies. During those 3 months, I have experienced a steep learning curve. I was confronted with other ways of working, other types of organisations and new challenges. These sort of experiences make you grow, both personally and professionally. Considering the extent of that growth, I believe the considerable investment made by my company was worthwhile. Changing context was a fabulous way to make me challenge the status quo, coming back to my practice with fresh ideas on how to do my work. It also made me feel my company was a great place to work and that they wanted to provide me with a special recognition.

Obviously, there are some drawbacks to this program. Some people liked their experience so much that they never came back. There is a real danger of losing good and experienced people. Having said that, if I had to commit to a certain number of years at the company, but did not want to be there, would I have done my work as well as previously? Probably not. Would frustration have had led to unwanted behaviours? Maybe.

Now, you may wonder, if I learned so much during this experience, how come I did not stay in that field? Well, I realised during that experience that doing meaningful work is not all for me. Meaning is a necessary but not sufficient condition. In addition to finding meaning in what I do, I love the excitement that I get when exchanging with top leaders, it is important for me to lead large, complex programs, with international reach. I also appreciate working for an innovative organisation that enables me to deliver quality work. I want to work in a fun environment where different opportunities exist. I need to work in a job and for an organisation which support and reflect my identity. More importantly, I got to realise that I do not need to work for an NGO to do good, and that in reality, the dark side of NGOs is much larger than I originally expected.

To Conclude: On the importance of the decision to engage

"Most folks are as happy as they make up their minds to be"
Abraham Lincoln (1809-1865)

What I see when looking at the client organisations I work with is an increasingly competent HR practice. The HR function has changed significantly in the last two decades. We now have an HR population which does not solely focus on administrative tasks but rather, become change agents, and do their best in order to attract, retain and develop the best talent. Having worked with a multitude of executive committees, I have seen leaders increasingly convinced by the importance of engaging their people. Organisations, increasingly, create the conditions for employees to strive. What I observe however, are employees representing a barrier to their own success and happiness. They come across as resisting to engage.

I see a high level of resistance to change, as well as an extremely low level of confidence in the fact that they have a real opportunity to change the way things are done and impact the organisation's culture and their daily routine. There is little sense that they can truly impact their organisation. People and organisations are okay with modifying or adding on existing processes, but it is really challenging to go back to the roots of a problem and feel you are 'allowed' to change things that are profoundly embedded in the way the organisation functions.

It is incredibly hard for people to feel their work environment is also theirs; that they are, as well as their leaders or managers, responsible for making it a better place to work. It is likely linked to the fact that culturally, in western countries at least, we have created hierarchical organisations, with layers, titles, and grades. What may allow me to fully invest in my company is that, to a certain extent, I personally feel responsible for making things happen. One element fostering this I believe comes down to the DNA of an organisation and in my case, the way my company defines its culture.

Where I work, the employee experience has been defined along ten key principles. Some of those 'principles' clearly emphasise autonomy, initiatives and does not really call for a hierarchical functioning. When those principles were first shared in the organisation, they strongly resonated with us, probably because they emerged from a series of short interviews with employees, and that the sampling was representing the rest of our workforce well. Those actually reflect our culture. We do not have strong hierarchies in place, but we have connections, friends. We are not waiting for opportunities to knock at our doors, but experience tells us that we need to be proactive in finding them. We take the initiative to make things happen, for us as for our clients. Having this freedom is exciting and motivating.

I see this sense of empowerment, often lacking in the organisations we work with. Obviously, this is easier for a company of 3,000 employees than one of 30,000. Still, when it comes to the new generation now joining organisations, I would expect they would require a greater degree of empowerment than in the past.

I recently watched the movie 'Jobs', in which Steve Jobs role was saying something along those lines: 'it only takes to realise that most things around us have been created by people no smarted than you, and that you can make it better'. That appears to me as applicable to all aspects of life.

Organisations, leaders and managers can create the conditions for employees to engage and to feel good about working somewhere but ultimately, this is a decision that employees have to make for themselves. As an employee, your state of mind will very much determine your experience of the workplace. We should not put the entire responsibility down to organisations or to a certain layer within those organisations. We should decide whether we want to make the most of the experience or not, and whether we are willing to invest our time, energy and intellect in changing our immediate surroundings for the better. As I said earlier, I believe this often starts with finding the right fit.

In that regard, to better understand the relationship between employees and employers, one could use the metaphor of personal relationships. As a teenager and young adult, one goes through several experiences, establishing relationships with various and often very different people. This process facilitates the discovery and identification of one's needs, help explore one's own identity as we grow and develop, until we meet the right person, who creates that desire to engage and commit on the long term. Similarly, employees may 'meet' a few organisations while growing into their practice, identifying who they are and what working environment they strive in, until they find the right organisation for them, which creates that desire to engage and commit long term. The challenge here is both people and organisations change and for the relationship to last, both will need to be willing to go towards the same direction, or part. Antoine de Saint Execupéry once wrote that 'love does not consist in gazing at each other, but in looking outwards together in the same direction'. This recipe for long term relationship happiness may just as well apply to organisations.

So, do I feel wedded to my organisation? Yes, to a certain extent. I am very much attached to the place, I feel mutual respect, trust is well anchored in our relationship, I can see now that we've had quite a journey together and I have tender feelings towards those memories. In summary, a good match has been found, and I have decided to fully engage with it; and I still see a bright future for us.

Now, I have to mention that my company has been acquired by a larger organisation. On the day the acquisition was completed, our CEO organised a meeting with all employees and started by 'today, our organisation has died'. I cried.

Discussing the narrative with Greg Kuzdenyi

"You can't get full engagement if people don't feel they are getting something out of it as well. Whenever I do something, I want the other person to win as much as I do, if not more."

A few words on Greg

Greg has worked as a technology Product Manager for five years in the UK. He led the design and development for the online proposition for one of the big name entertainment brands and has delivered a handful of products effecting millions of households.

Greg is also a passionate entrepreneur. He is currently setting up an enterprise aiming at helping property developers turn commercial properties into residential homes.

Greg has been living most of his life in the UK but his family's roots originate in Hungary.

Interview transcripts

Greg Kuzdenyi (GK): I was thinking of the questions you sent me and I came up with 3 reasons why I want to start my own company, and why I'm not satisfied with being an employee.

In no particular order: the first is money, because I am not satisfied with the salary ranges that employers give you, in relation to the demands of life. There is a discrepancy there.

The second is that I feel I want to do more in the world than just make someone else's product. I feel that I am limiting myself. I feel limited by the culture in the company, the people I work with, by the politics, etcetera. The bigger the company the more layers, the more bureaucracy, more people want to get their own personalities in the mix and it becomes managing people rather than getting a great product out the door. At the end of it, I find that very limiting.

And thirdly, I just got the feeling that I am not meant to do it. Leaving this earth, I want to look back and say 'wow, that guy made a difference'; to have more of an impact on the world we live in.

Interviewer: Greg, sorry to stop you there but before we get further into this, could you give me a bit of background on what you do?

GK: Well, we left the LSE at the end of 2007, which means that the big recession hit, as soon as we came out of school, it was the start of it all. I started to apply for graduate schemes. The reason why I did psychology for my undergraduate studies, before LSE, was because I was fascinated by it. That has been a common thread in my life, I go for what I am interested in, not necessarily what I am good at. I have the opinion that if you are interested, you work harder and you get good at it.

So, that was probably the biggest reason why I did psychology out of school. I had never done it before but I was fascinated by how the human brain works, why certain people, in the same situation, doing the same thing, can get different results. After my undergraduates, I knew I had to specialise in something which would allow me to work afterwards, and decided to do Organisational Psychology. It was a perfect fit for me, as human interactions was my interest. By the end of it however I thought, 'I actually don't want to do it full time, 5 days a week, for the rest of my life'. I still wanted to continue along the lines of psychology somehow, today still I read about psychology almost every single day, but I thought 'what do I actually want to do Monday to Friday?'. My other passion being technology, I applied for a bunch of technology graduate roles, from technology consulting in Accenture, all the way to a pure technology program where you learn development, testing, and so on. I probably applied to about 50 different jobs. I then got accepted on the technology graduate scheme at my current company. It is for 2 years, 4 times 6 month roles. One was Development, which, at that point I'd thought I'll never do. The second was testing, Quality Assurance, which I again thought I will never do but was interesting to learn. The other was Operational Consulting, how the department runs. The last one, which I went into the graduate scheme with a mind to do, was Business Analysis. That is all around what drives the business requirements, where do they come from, how do you come up with them, how do you work out the benefits and value and the whole process of how do you make the end products. They took 12 people on, 6 had a background in technology, and they took 6 people from an arty background like history, arts or psychology. The reason they do this is to balance out left brainers and right brainers, so are you more analytical thinking or do you think more abstract and creatively. I actually nearly became a developer, which was as much a surprise to me as I think it is a surprise to you. I just loved it so much, it was probably the hardest 6 months I've done, because I worked, and took my work home and programmed some more, just because I loved it.

Interviewer: Interesting, it seems to contradict what you were saying on how you have made your choices so far, which was about your passion and not your capacity.

GK: Yes, initially I choose what I do by what I really enjoy but then when I do it, if I don't do it to very high standards, I do not enjoy it any longer, and end up not doing it anymore. I don't see the point of doing something if it is not done well.

I went on doing Business Analysis, I got a job there. When working in Business Analysis, that's when I saw the job I wanted to do, the one I am doing right now. A business analyst takes the requirements from a Product Manager and turns them into technical language. They are the gate keepers between business and technology. They are the people which need to understand the way developers think and talk as well as the way business people think and talk. They take business talk and turn it into technical talk and think through the whole process of what needs to happen. When I started the Business Analysis job, I actually saw that Product Management was what I wanted to do. It is a bit more creative, it is more on the business side. The way I look at it is, you've got 3 different levels: a Technical Analyst, who is 80% technical, 20% business; the Business Analyst who must be 50/50;

and the Product Manager who is 80% business and 20% technical. I knew I wanted to be a Product Manager because, and I suppose, it comes down to 3 things here again, I wanted the freedom, and the possibility to think 'how do we build this product the best way that we can, how do we add the most value, how do we do this the most efficient way', and I was able to do that when I was a business analysis in suggesting ideas to the product manager, but it was just my suggestion against his decision. Naturally, I was constantly suggesting things. I did not realise I was doing it but apparently I was. When the Product Manager left, she recommended me for her role, without me even knowing anything about it. Now, I have been doing product management for the last year.

About 2 years ago I started my own company on the side. I've always wanted to do this as I had a fascination about it. I think it was actually the LSE which sparked something off because it has a very self-motivated start up culture. The people that go to the LSE are very motivated people, go getters, 'let's get the most out of life' type of people, and that environment sparked it off. I've never done anything like this before, I have not gone into business before, so I've been attending start-up courses learning about how to build a company, how do you do everything from marketing to accounting, business models to broader things that you need to know. I also got myself a business mentor. I launched my first company, which was a speech therapy agency. Again, I went off the basis of what I enjoy, and what I am good at, and it is a big personal thing for me. I've started to stammer when I was about 7 or 8. It was very pronounced in school, I could hardly say 3 or 4 words at a time, so that was a very difficult part of my life to go through, and then as I gained more confidence, the speech started to flow a lot more. Even to this day, I still stammer, you probably can't hear it because I've become better at controlling it. After a lot of thought and soul searching on what to do, it took me about 6 months to decide on that idea, and it was only because somebody in the course stood up with their business idea, and she was a speech therapist, that I thought I could do something like that too. Once I decided that this was what I wanted to do, I started to think about the practicalities, 'how do I do this?'. I have not done speech therapy, I was given speech therapy so I know what it is like from a client perspective but not from a practitioners' perspective. I got myself a speech therapist mentor and started practicing; I got myself a psychology mentor too. This is controversial in the speech therapy industry but my personal opinion is that a stammer is 95% psychology and 5% actually technique. Some people seem to think it is genetics, some think it is habitual, there is a lot of debate and nobody actually knows what causes stammering. There is a big debate about it. Anyhow, I studied speech therapy, as well as psychology, which grew me as a person. It changed my life in the way I approach things. I helped adolescents, late teens to twenties, and my plan was to stop doing that and go to schools to teach young children because that is when therapy is the most effective. I did it before work and after work and at weekends.

About 1 month ago I started to get practical about it. I got lost into the 'Oh my God, this is amazing, I'm going to change people's lives and make money at the same time, it's going to be really meaningful since I've gone through it myself'. I realised that most speech therapist did not have a stammer and thought it was perfect, this was my calling. But about 1 month ago, I started having a look at it properly and reflected on why I was doing this and on those 3 elements that I mentioned at the beginning: I just want my own business – I feel it is the right thing for me to do, I feel that is my calling – the second one to make money and to support myself and my future family, and that is actually the bit that got to me. My plan was that when I will earn as much with my own business as in my current job, then I will leave my job. Until then I don't want to leave. At the time we just bought a flat, we now have a mortgage; my wife really wanted to leave her job and was in danger of being made redundant, so there were all those pressures for me to stay in my job as long as I could. I asked myself: 'Can I really get enough money from this job per month and how quickly can I get up to my current salary?', and it was not feasible to do it quick enough, or to do it at the level I wanted to. So I made a tough choice last month, to stop doing that for now, to delay it, and do something that will take less time to make money and once I have made the money, I can come back to that.

Interviewer: So in terms of ranking priorities it sounds like, quite understandingly, money is the basic which needs to be in place and drives the practicalities of things, a fundamental that needs to be answered.

GK: Yes, absolutely. And those values change overtime as well. I started this off in a dream, I thought this was going to be great, I'll do what I am called to do and really want to do, what I feel passionate about and money will come later on. I did not really look at it practically. I then got to a point where I had to look at it practically because it was not flourishing as quickly as I wanted to. We are in an age in our lives where there are many things that we want to do and you need a lot of money for that. Practically, I decided to delay that.

I am now launching a new idea: it is marketing and building websites and services for a particular industry niche, and the reasoning behind that is first that my current job is to do with online, I know it very well. I did it because not only am good at it but I have a passion for technology and giving users a better experience. The plan is to establish myself in the UK first and then continue with the same niche in different countries. I am doing a lot of sales training at the moment, because I'll be doing the face to face selling, I'll be talking to clients about the value we add, the problems we solve for them.

Interviewer: Now, coming on linking to the narrative, if you think about the notion of engagement, what does that look like for you?

GK: I see two things here, how I would do engagement as an entrepreneur, and what I see at my current company. So, there are different types of engagement. There is engagement on a cultural level: do you feel that you fit into the culture of the team and the wider department? Then there is engagement on the level of your physical surroundings: do you actually enjoy going to work and where you work, your work environment? There is engagement from the perspective of reward: do you feel that the work you do gets adequately rewarded? Formal recognition, coming from your salary and bonuses, as well as intangible ones: praise from your manager, the reason you are doing something, what difference does that make, the values of your company, does that match up with your own values, etcetera.

Interviewer: And what does that mean to you?

GK: Engagement to me, in the context of my current company, which is different from my own company, comes down to the fact that I love the products I work on, I am proud of what we are doing, I am proud of what we have done so far but mainly proud of where we are heading. Our products add value to many people, and that is important to me. It is making a difference, even if it means a small difference to a lot of people. To me that is a big difference in total. I also appreciate what the company values: innovation, thinking outside of the box, and not stopping getting better, continually improving.

Recognition from a formal point of view I don't support. I don't like the pay or bonus structure, it does not adequately reward people. I don't think they really think through their staff at a human level. They think of them as 'you are number 137', and if you are not needed, you are not needed. But that comes down to the big culture, you become more a number than an individual at a macro level. In your team, obviously you remain an individual but the decisions around reward are made higher in the organisation. But that is the opposite of engaging.

The people I work with I enjoy a lot. It's the same type of people you would find at LSE in terms of they are very motivated to get things done, they are very analytical. It is a very small team, it is 5 of us but we are all very entrepreneurial in the sense that we like to think of new ideas and see if that would add value and try to put that into a service.

I do like the company's vision, the whole vision is 'Believe in Better' and I like that because of the continuous improvement and whatever product they do, they try to put that in. I do believe in the broader company vision, but in the meantime, I am more attached to the actual products. I think that's natural. I don't think it is healthy, or natural to attach your self-worth or identity to something outside of you though. What I am not saying is don't put yourself into your work as much as you can, and do the best you can with everything you have. What I am saying is, do that, but at the end of the day, if it does not work, don't let that identify your worth.

Now launching my new company, what I have learnt is not to do everything myself. I have tried to do everything myself in my first company and it is probably the main reason why I was not getting as much traction in it. I have tried to be the sales person, the therapist, the marketer, everybody! This is what you get taught to do and need to do to a certain extent when you start off but one of the crucial success factors I identified was I should outsource as much as I could, apart from 3 core things: sales, marketing and innovation & creativity. I've now gone with a model organised around 3 core activities that I do myself and I outsource everything else. I have got contractors, a whole team. The way I like to look at it is that if you are to engage people, you need to build trust with them. So you need to be open, you need to be truthful to them, just be transparent with what you do. The more transparent, the more truthful you are, the more trust you build, the more foundation there is for your relationship with them. So, that is one of the key elements. The other key thing I find is 'win-win'. I don't think you can get full engagement with somebody if they don't feel they are getting something out of it as well. So, whenever I do something, I want the other person to win as much as I do, if not more. When somebody feels rewarded and engaged, they will do an exponential amount more than if they don't feel engaged and rewarded. Trust and win-win are the two key factors I see.

As an employee, it is very important for me to grow but some people don't care. I think it is up to the person to either want or not want to make it happen. I am very supportive of growth because I want to grow myself, but I am not going to push them. First because I don't have the time; and second because if I do something instead of them, I am actually taking something away from them, not making them grow. So it is important for me but ultimately it is their decision.

Probably the biggest thing I've learnt last year is to do with our experience of life in general. There are 3 levels of how people experience life, and let's keep it to the company context so we can relate to it. The first type of experience is to question where do our experiences come from. Experience is situational, people tie their experiences to the situation or context they are in. Taking an example, if I am at work and I have a really bad day, if that is consistent, I start associating that situation – being at work – with feeling bad. That is the initial, and most basic way to look at it.

The second level is to question how our experiences drive our behaviours, and how we empower ourselves in responding to a given situation. There are two ways people actually do that, they either motivate or protect themselves. Going into 'protecting' and taking the example of a situation where I feel fear, let's say that I am really scared of talking to my manager, in order to protect myself, I will then avoid talking to him as much as possible. In a 'motivating' mode, people will do things to get to something else. A great example is money. A lot of financially successful people get burnt out because they are motivated by financial scarcity; they are scared to be broke, so they do everything not to be broke.

The level which changed my life, the third one, is realising where our experiences comes from. So, at the most basic level, you would say 'in that situation, I get scared', then you either motivate or protect yourself, but then the question is 'where does that fear actually come from?'. When you look at it, it is not the situation you are in, it is not the people you are with, it is not the culture, the context, anything! It is your thinking about the situation which drives it. The way experience works is that you have a constant stream of thoughts flowing through your head, never ending from birth to death. It is extremely difficult to switch it off. Every single thought has a feeling attached to it. You cannot have a thought without a feeling and it is that flow of thoughts that you experience with your feelings going up and down during the day. You could be in the worst job, doing the worst thing and you can have the time of your life and feel perfectly fine. This is more than empowering yourself.

What I am saying is that actually, you do not have a decision. You can't decide what you will be thinking about in the future, constantly. And if you can't decide what you will be thinking in the future, you cannot decide how you will feel in the future. Then it appears futile to try to control your own feelings. So, it is about seeing that and accepting that whatever is going through your mind, and however long it takes, a second, a minute, an hour, a day, a week, a month, a year, that will change. It is almost going back to no control. You can nurture positive or negative thinking, you can train yourself to think positively but that is tiring and not going naturally with how our minds are set up to work. But when you realise that what you feel is your thinking, this is when you can just let go. This helps a lot at work. Whenever I start feeling stressed, overwhelmed, instead of taking me hours to calm down, I catch it as soon as I start to feel it and I realise what is going on and it dissolves itself.

Interviewer: Coming back to your own organisation, I would like to ask you, what leader would you like to be?

GK: It is one thing to be thinking about what sort of leader you would like to be and another actually being that leader. It is very difficult to see yourself from an outside perspective. If I wanted to describe what kind of leader I would like to be, the core things for me are to be transparent, truthful and trustworthy. The other is being inspirational in the sense that I would like others to see what I do and be inspired by that more than by what I say. I would like to enable people to get more of themselves by working with me. Quality: whatever I do, it has to be of quality. I don't believe in selling something that is not the best that I can do. I just want people to enjoy what they do with me, and want to have fun, a lot of fun! I want work to be play and play to be work. I am struggling with this at the moment, but what is work/life balance? And is there such a thing? The more I think about it, the more I think there is no work/life balance but rather, work/life integration. You bring your life into your work and your work into your life. As an entrepreneur, I don't believe in working from 9 to 5 and then doing something else. I believe in getting the people around you on-board with what you are doing.

Interviewer: What kind of employees would you like to have?

GK: Just the same thing. The more behaviours we share, the better. We will then work as a team better. The one thing is, I will not work with someone not truthful, honest and transparent. If they are, I will forgive anything else.

Interviewer: Now, thinking about our generation at work, and comparing with previous generations in the workplace, do you see vast differences in terms of behaviours?

GK: The only difference I see, and what everybody talks about right now, is that Gen X are much more focused on a long term career. They'll go in a company, will want to settle down in that company, go up the ladder, and look for stability. Whereas, Gen Y are more free spirited, generally we do many things at the same time, watching TV, while on our phones, while talking to people, we are multitasked. I feel we are more creative with less attention span.

Interviewer: And if we try to decipher the myth from reality?

GK: That's a good point. So what do I actually see? I see a lot of people within my current employer's company move very quickly. They are at the boundary between our generation and Gen X. An average job at my current company has, maybe a 2 year lifespan. That is also linked to the fact that we work with a lot of contractors. The nature of the contracting job is much more sporadic.

Interviewer: OK. Another question for you: What have you seen at your current company that you would not like to see in your own business?

GK: What we do really badly, especially in my department, especially in my team is time management in terms of identify priorities and urgencies, that matrix of importance on one axis and urgency on the other. Do we do the most urgent less important first? Yes. Or do we do the most important less urgent first? No. It is hugely swayed one way. We don't get any time to think about the future, you really have to fight for that. There is little in terms of stopping and thinking about what is going well or not. That is a huge thing I would like to change. And I suppose, treating people for people, and not just their job title or the number HR give them. There is an important gap between us and the higher levels of the organisation, and that is not something I would like to repeat.

Interviewer: What culture would you like to build?

GK: What I believe is that the culture gets built by the people that are there. And that also comes back to the question of what leader I would like to be. And what I said around leadership is what I would like in terms of culture: Honesty, transparency, openness, willingness to be better every day, innovation, creativity, focus on quality, fun, focus on relationships with people. With the culture at my current company, there is a good fit between me and my team, but it is only 5 of us. It is actually difficult to find people which fit into our team because we are so similar in the way we work. I think I am a good fit with the department, but the fit is easier there, it is bigger, you have variations, and I find it even easier to fit in the company, as it has a huge amount of variations in terms of people. I do feel I am a good fit. I do like working for them, but there is this spark in me, willing to do more, that is not there with my colleagues and that is why I feel I need to go. If I did not have that spark, I think it would be great. But because I have it, I just can't see myself staying in the long term. And that makes me not fit.

Interviewer: Greg, we are coming at the end of our time together. Anything else you'd like to add?

GK: No, I think that's it! Thank you.

Postface: A few words to conclude

I see no hope for the future of our people if they are dependent on frivolous youth of today, for certainly all youth are reckless beyond words... When I was young, we were taught to be discreet and respectful of elders, but the present youth are exceedingly wise [disrespectful] and impatient of restraint.

Hesiod (ca. 700 BC)

Categorisation's pitfall

It seems that Hesiod's perception of youth at his time has travelled through ages, and that we still regularly hear today similar judgements on younger generations. This raises the question of whether or not the situation has continuously gone downhill for the last 2500+ years. Alternatively, we may want to consider that our history shows a tendency to be slightly alarmist regarding youngsters' behaviours, and that we have generally been confusing how people behave with what they deeply believe in.

Should we distinguish between the notion of 'practices', which are actions very much anchored in the environment we evolve in, and our deeper beliefs and values? The former would generally be more volatile than the latter. Beliefs and values are deeply planted into each individual and ultimately drive their attitudes and behaviours. What I see in the workplace today, and what many of our contributors hinted towards is that while practices vary across age groups in the workplace, values may not be fluctuating as much as we think. Notions such as security, respect, or passion have come through those narratives and interviews, and do not seem to me as being solely owned by any generation.

Now referring to the notions Edgar Schein (1992)[38] used in his work on organisational culture, we see that in our particular group of contributors, the basic assumptions in the culture that they convey remain quite steady (I.e. work structures our lives and provides a sense of meaning), values are slowly shifting (i.e. more focus on empowerment) while it is actually artefacts which vary to a great extent (i.e. technology and connectedness).

Now, what we see today with people being more connected, multi-tasking, or collaborative are what we would call 'practices'. Younger people entering the workplace would acquire new habits – or practices – having none to erase beforehand, while an older workforce has already acquired many which may be more difficult to shift. Kurt Lewin's (1947)[39] change model has shown that to change behaviours individuals should first 'unfreeze' their previous behaviour, change it and finally 'refreeze' the new behaviour. From this perspective, new comers to the workplace would then have one less adoption step as they would not have to 'unfreeze' previously acquired behaviours. As a consequence - putting aside

[38] Schein, E. (1992). Organisational culture and leadership. London: Jossey-Bass.
[39] Lewin, K. (1947). Forces behind food habits and methods of change. Bulletin of the National Research Council, 108, 35-65.

levels of resistance to change, and individuals' willingness to adapt - we can expect that the acquisition of those new practices for tenured employees is a question of time rather than generations per se.

This raises a more important question: Is there really any Gen Y, X or Baby-boomers? Reading through those young professionals' narratives and interviews I start doubting that that is the case at all. There seems to be some superficiality in creating those categories. Is someone born in 1976 going to be fundamentally different from someone born in 1982? It is very likely, as would be the case for two people with two different lives and backgrounds born on the same day. Would any common characteristics come purely from the generation they belong to? I would rather argue that as our societies evolve, the way we experience work does too. The general flexibility and nimbleness required to do business today force changes in hierarchies, structures and processes which all of us have no choice but to embrace. Some might be more drawn to change than others, however, and as argued above, this may partly stem from the fact that some may have fewer practices to get rid of before acquiring new ones.

Two weeks ago, my sister, her husband, their three kids, my partner and I all took a plane down to South of France to surprise our Dad on the day of his 70th birthday. I took the opportunity during the flight to do some reading on new trends in managerial practices, and as I was reviewing some of the characteristics typically attributed to the Generation Y - and the challenges in managing them - I realised that my 70 year-old Dad is probably the best incarnation of Gen Y I know. Coming to this fact, I can only challenge the inherent relevance of those generational categories.

As a matter of fact, all contributors of this book graduated in the late 2000s, as would students from the Generation Y, and clearly, do give accounts of their working lives around – and to pick only a couple of points - a search for meaning, a need for flexibility, being focused on the wider contribution, however, some were born in the 70s. Should we then consider them as representatives of Generation X? Are those generations a question of mind-set rather than a fact? I would go for the former.

I understand how those categories may be useful in analysing workplaces and practices. I believe however that one should be extremely careful in applying this lens to look at people and organisations as they tend to come attached with prejudices and may misguide us. Using those categories with care then, let's recap on what we heard in the stories and personal accounts shared earlier in this book, and highlight what seems to emerge consistently throughout.

Searching for meaning

The notion of meaning has come through very strongly, and has done so with different facets: one more internal, revolving around the work itself and its impact on us, and one more external, touching on elements going far beyond work but closer to society and the wider impact of the act of working.

The internal meaning refers to the fact that work structures our lives, it gives purpose and it makes 'sense' to work, it creates a certain routine. Work helps us feel useful. Additionally, it appears still today to play a social role in terms of status and external image. This perception of work is fairly traditional and not particularly surprising, even for the so-called Gen Y. The external facet of meaning however is typically more attached to young professionals today and has indeed emerged as the number one concern for our contributors. Here, we touch on the personal responsibility that a company takes to be a responsible organisation and to contribute to a greater good. Many contributors want to shape a society where social good and business are fully integrated, where we can do business in a socially responsible way, as well as working for social enterprises which are financially sound and independent.

Our conversations around meaning revealed that meaning can be found in various ways. It is a perspective to take rather than a stated fact. It appears clear as well that it is not because one works for an NGO that the work performed would be particularly meaningful. It would very much depend on how an organisation behaves, and the perspective one takes in approaching the day to day work.

When reflecting on this notion of meaning recently, I kept on coming back to the example of people working on making our technology based communications possible. When fixing a telephone line for instance, one may think that this is not the most exciting job when looking at it through the lens of the actual work that is conducted. But if we take a step back and think about what it actually means to the wider community, it changes the picture. A man fixing a damaged cable is not just fixing that cable but also enables potentially isolated people to reconnect to the world, call for help if needed, or just receive a call from loved ones and bring a moment of joy. The point here is that meaning does not come from the type of work one does but rather the way work is performed and the perspective taken while working. I recently came across an old business parable related to this. It goes as follow: Three stone cutters were asked about their work. As the first answered he was paid to cut stones, the second replied that he used special techniques to shape stones in an exceptional way. The third stone cutter just smiled and said 'I build cathedrals'. Of course, taking a perspective bringing a sense of meaning to work is not always possible, but often it is. This is where it is so crucial that the leaders of an organisation state a strong vision and mission statement employees can relate to, and help them to connect with the bigger picture.

Intentionality

The second notion which came across very strongly in our narratives and interviews is the one of intentionality. The notion of intentionality in the context of our working lives refers to our willingness, as workers, to make the most of that experience, and be active actors in that setting. Intentionality is tightly intertwined with the notion of empowerment and the extent to which organisations allow for that attitude to emerge. Our contributors are proactive in shaping their working lives, they want to make their own decisions and be autonomous. In other words, they intentionally steer their working lives. But that is only possible because the context in which they live has evolved too, and today, such an approach is encouraged and recognised. Organisations increasingly create the conditions for employees to feel greatly empowered and involved in decision making processes.

Conversations on the importance of reshaping organisations and the culture they reinforce have started a long time ago. After having watched an inspiring talk on TED.com by Ricardo Semler on the way he has pushed and supported the transformation of the organisation that his father had founded, I ordered the book he had written almost 25 years ago[40]. In this book he tells the story of Semco, and the radical changes it has undergone in the transition from his father's management to his, moving from a traditional autocratic style of management to a decentralised and participative one. In other words, moving from a setting where intentionality is not an option, to one where it is encouraged. He also details the exponential growth Semco went through following that cultural change. When Ricardo Semler explains what those changes meant in practice, this is a faithful description of the organisation 2.0 which is portrayed everywhere today. But this was 25 years ago. Luckily, it seems that since, the good word has spread.

The chance of magic

Many contributors have, indirectly, stressed the large proportion of unknown in our lives, and hence, working lives. What I gathered from the stories shared by our contributors is that the ability to weather ambiguity and uncertainly builds resilience, helps keep a positive look and allows one to remain open to unexpected moments of magic. Anticipation can go a long way, but is ultimately limited. From our limited anticipation powers both difficulties and challenges could emerge, as much as positive

[40] Semler, R. (1993). Maverick! : The Success Story Behind the World's Most Unusual Workplace: Grand Central Publishing.

experiences or a bit of magic. If we cannot anticipate magic, it is because it is greatly down to luck, it comes by chance, thanks to the happy alignment of a few fundamental elements.

When magic has been discussed in earlier narratives and interviews, it indeed seemed to be particularly attached to elements out of our control, such as personal relationships and the social aspects of the day to day at work. It appears to be about the 'space in between', the intangible of interactions, the impalpable. An organisation may be able to create the conditions for magic to sparkle - studying the composition of teams and team dynamics for example - but an organisation's power to create magical moments for their employees is ultimately constrained.

Uncontrollable, magic is nonetheless crucial in bringing positivity to the workplace and supporting employees' attachment to it. It is interesting to note that magic is one of the fundamentals we have minimum power on.

Play at work

Play: *'engage in activity for enjoyment and recreation rather than a serious or practical purpose'*. This is not a word I expected to hear frequently when discussing working patterns with my fellow LSE alumni. It has however come up in numerous instances. More than the reality of play at work, it is the wish for more play at work which emerged, and the belief that this is the way forward to increase creativity, engagement and productivity in organisations. Some literature seems to corroborate this perspective, probably explaining the increasing presence of 'serious games' at work.

It is interesting to witness the entrance of gaming into the workplace. It is not positioned as a method which would need to be embedded in the day to day work, in a company's DNA, but rather as a method to be used for problem solving, personal development or learning, in a very well defined setting. It becomes a process rather than a cultural component. Hence, the message conveyed is that we can and should play at work, but in a structured way. Is play supposed to be that way? Is that really what is going to bring about true innovation and respond to the need for creativity a few of our contributors expressed?

A key feature of the act of playing is that we typically play with and against other people. What would be the impact of this new method on competition which so frequently shapes games on playgrounds? How does that support our need for more collaborative ways of working?

Many see this trend of incrementally bringing more play at work but we still have to collectively figure out how this would work and what would the impact be on both people and organisations.

Trust at large

The last thread that I would like to highlight here is the one of trust. When we have been discussing earlier work patterns and balance with our personal life, empowerment, latitude in decision making and so many other topics, I believe this is trust we were discussing: trust in ourselves, mutual trust with our colleagues, our organisations and our societies; confidence that we will finally understand the misery of the short term perspectives too frequently favoured and appreciate the necessity of finally seeing our actions in a wider framework; trust in mankind, our ability to evolve and our ultimate hope for a better future.

Many of our contributors are optimists and want to make this world a better place to live and a better place to work – how idealistic and romantic of us some would say. So maybe we have not joined the LSE by fluke as 120 years ago, the school was founded by Graham Wallas, Sidney Webb, Beatrice Webb and Georges Bernard Shaw for *'the betterment of society'*. This vision appears to still be distilled and carried by some of its students.

So here we are: A group of 10 young professionals, taking on the journey of our working lives and reflecting on it. On that journey, we are still on the platform, just stepping a foot on the train we wish to get on board to. We know the general direction, not sure yet where it will stop or how long the journey will be. What seems certain is that we want to contribute to making the journey more interesting and enjoyable.

Ann-Victoire Pincé

Opening up the conversation

One of the key focuses in the journey we have taken with *From Millennials With Love* is that we wanted to exchange and open up, create a platform for a conversation. If you wish to, feel free to come on www.frommillennialswithlove.com to comment our narratives and interviews, ask questions or challenge us. We would like to hear from you.

* 9 7 8 1 7 8 4 5 6 2 4 7 2 *

ND - #0177 - 060826 - C0 - 197/132/16 - PB - 9781784562472 - Matt Lamination